WHAT'S UP WITH MY LIFE?

Finding And Living Your True Purpose

GAIL THACKRAY

Copyright © 2015 Gail Thackray

All rights reserved. No part of this book may be reproduced or transmitted in any form or by any means, electronic or mechanical, including photocopying, recording, or by any information storage and retrieval system without written permission of the publisher, except for the inclusion of brief quotations in a review.

The purpose of the book is to educate and entertain. The author is providing techniques, suggestions, tips, and ideas intended for your emotional and spiritual wellbeing but the author is not a professional in the fields of finance, career or other subjects covered in this book. The author and publisher shall have neither liability nor responsibility to anyone with respect to any loss or damage caused or alleged to be caused, directly or indirectly, by the information contained in this book.

Printed in the United States of America

Thackray, Gail

    What's Up with My Life? Finding and Living Your True Purpose /by Gail Thackray

ISBN: 978-0-9861338-0-0

Edited by Mara Krausz
Layout and Design by Teagarden Designs
Author photograph by Kevin Ellsworth

Published by
Indian Springs Publishing
P.O. Box 286
La Cañada, CA 91012
www.indianspringspublishing.com

DO YOU ABSOLUTELY LOVE YOUR LIFE?

IS YOUR LIFE FULFILLING AND EXCITING WITH GREAT RELATIONSHIPS, PERFECT HEALTH, THE IDEAL JOB, AND FILLED WITH ABUNDANCE?

ARE YOU HAVING FUN?

IF NOT, THIS BOOK IS FOR YOU!

We are all born with a purpose–a mission in life, and when we know it and live it, life flows perfectly.

Author Gail Thackray guides you in answering:

- What is the meaning of my life?
- How can I identify my strengths and life tools?
- How can I more fully embrace my True Purpose?
- How can I turn my hobby into my dream job?
- How can I get rid of the blockages that are holding me back?
- Why do I keep repeating the same mistakes?
- How can I identify karma that may be holding me back?
- How can I have more prosperity in my life?

We are meant to live our True Purpose in abundance.
What is your passion, and what's stopping you from living your dream?

Practical tips and exercises for how to create a more fulfilling life.

Gail Thackray is an intuitive medium as well as a life coach. Gail has a gift for helping people to remove their blockages and discover their self-worth. In her book "30 Days to Prosperity: A Workbook to Manifest Abundance," Gail created an easy-to-follow program, which many report has brought them unexpected abundance. After leading a "normal" life, everything changed at age forty when she discovered that she was a medium and able to talk to the spirit world. Gail has a way of imparting spiritual guidance with a down-to-earth sensibility and sense of humor that will keep you enthralled.

CONTENTS

PART I: What is True Purpose? 9
  What Is the Meaning of My Life? 9
    Our Purpose Is Preordained 10
  Free Will 15
    We Have Free Will 15
    Health and Exit Points 18
  Karma, Themes, and Predetermined Aspects 19
    Karma 19
    Multiple Themes 23
    Divinely Orchestrated 24
    Predestined Family 25
    Multiple Dimensions 28
    The Waking Age 29
  Defining Your True Purpose 29
    Why Know Your True Purpose? 29
    No Competition 31
    The Process of Discovering 31
    The Influence of Others 32

PART II: Finding Your True Purpose 33
  Feeling Your True Purpose 33
    Guidance from Heaven 35
    Ask Your Guides about Your True Purpose 36
    Meditation Preparation 37
    Meet Your Guides and
    Discover Your True Purpose Meditation 37
  Life Tools 40
    Finding Your Life Tools 40
    Your Life Tools List 42
    Life Tool List – In Progress 43
  Exercises to Help Identify Your Life Tools 45
    Find Tools in Your Achievements 45
    Find Life Tools in the People You Admire 45
    Find Tools in What Others See in You 47
    Find Tools in Your Physical Attributes 49
    Find Tools in What Irks You about Others 50
    Find Tools in Your Faults 51

Find Tools in Your Fears	52
Find Tools in Your Relationships	54
Your Final Life Tools List	55
Themes	56
Finding Your Themes	56
Your Themes List	56
Sample Themes	56
Exercises to Help Identify Your Themes	59
Find Themes in a Negative Condition	59
Find Themes in Your Major Life Moments	60
Find Themes in Positive Life Events	62
Find Themes in Negative Life Events	63
Themes in Your Relationships	65
Themes in What Irks You about Others	66
Themes in When People Ask You for Help	66
Find Themes in Your Past Projects	67
Find Themes in Your Perfect Job	68
Find Themes in Your Interests	69
Your Final Themes List	69
Your True Purpose Statement	70
True Purpose Statement Examples	72
My True Purpose is	72
Test the Truth of Your True Purpose Statement	75
Does Your True Purpose Match Your Map?	75
Astrology and Your True Purpose	76
The North Node	76
North and South Node Table	77
How the Sign of Your North and South Node Affects You	80
Numerology and Your True Purpose	85
Simple Birth Number	85
True Purpose Number	86
Numerology of Your Name	89
The Vibrational Meaning of Numbers	90
Does Your Astrology and Numerology Fit Your True Purpose?	94
Final True Purpose Statement	95
Your True Purpose Statement	95
My True Purpose Statement is:	95
True Purpose in Your Job and Activities	96

- How Are You Currently Living Your True Purpose? 96
  - True Purpose through Career 97
  - The 80/20 Rule 98
  - Should I Quit My Job? 99
  - In-between Jobs? 101
  - Baby Steps 102
  - Your True Purpose in Your Hobbies and Activities 104
  - Check That Your True Purpose Is Actually Yours 104
- Releasing Obstacles 106
  - Dictated by Circumstance 106
  - I've Made a Bunch of Mistakes 107
  - What Is Holding You Back? 108
- Past Life Blockages 111
  - Past Life Regression 111
  - Examples of blocks and fears – Client Sessions 111
  - Dan 111
  - Jenny 112
  - Dillon 113
- Past Life Meditation to Discover your Blocks 114
- Past Life Meditation 115
- Imagining Your True Purpose 118
  - Your Perfect Day 118
  - The Completion of Your Life 118
  - Gratitude in Your True Purpose 119
- In Support of Your True Purpose 120
  - Make Time for Your Purpose 120
  - You Deserve To Be Successful 121
  - You *Can* Make Money Doing What You Love 122
- It Is Yours by Divine Right 124
- Spiritual Help with Your True Purpose 125
- Meditation – Guide Me along My Path 125
- My New Life – Living My True Purpose 126
  - Action Points I Am Going To Do Right Now 127

Acknowledgments 129

About the Author 131

NOTHING FEELS MORE MAGICAL THAN WHEN YOUR LIFE FLOWS PERFECTLY. THAT IS LIVING YOUR TRUE PURPOSE.

PART I
WHAT IS TRUE PURPOSE?

WHAT IS THE MEANING OF MY LIFE?

Are we having fun yet? If not, then why? Sometimes there comes a point in our lives when we think, "What is my purpose?" or "What am I really doing here?" Oftentimes this comes at a breaking point when we are completely lost or about to give up. Sometimes we are lucky and contemplate this question long before falling into a slump of despair. The specific circumstances don't matter. If you've picked up this book, then you are probably asking the question, "Where am I going with my life?"

Our lives have meaning. No matter how small or insignificant we may think we are at this particular moment in time, we do have a purpose. We all have a very big, important purpose. Your life is significant and you have been chosen for a particular path and a grand role in the scheme of life; it's just that perhaps you are not sure what that is right now.

We've all had those times where everything just seems to flow, when we are enthusiastic, have drive and ambition, and know that we have a purpose in life. This is when we're on the right track. But then there are other times where we throw up our arms and say:

"What's up with my life?"

"What is this all about?"

"What am I doing here?"

This is when we may feel like we're on a hamster wheel just going day-to-day, doing our thing but not feeling like we are getting anywhere.

Perhaps you are in a job that pays the bills but that's about it; there is no real feeling of fulfillment, passion, or achievement. Perhaps you are dealing with financial challenges, health issues, or emotional stress. Maybe life has thrown you some difficult curveballs and juggling them is all you seem to do. All this can weigh you down, keeping you caught up in the minutia of daily life. Sometimes we are so busy putting out each little fire that it's hard to get ahead; responsibilities and difficulties are taking you down another path until you have gotten completely off track. If you're not paying attention, you can wander further and further away until you have completely forgotten why you are here in the first place.

• •

I am here to reiterate that you do have a purpose–a very big, important purpose! We are about to find out what that is and get you feeling and living your purpose! And, most of all, having fun!

• •

Our Purpose Is Preordained

I believe that we are each born with a True Purpose or destiny that is the theme we carry throughout our life. I find it hard to discuss one's Purpose or the meaning of life without talking about God, Divine Source, or the heavenly realms. Okay, I haven't gone all religious on you or anything. Don't worry if you don't share this belief or agree with me; it won't diminish the effectiveness of this workbook or the finding of your True Purpose. The exercises contained within will help you to discover your Purpose regardless of your religious or spiritual beliefs.

 I find that most people believe in the existence of a Higher Source, a higher guiding power, a Divine maker. Even if they don't give regular consideration to this belief, for many there is an underlying trust in Divine intervention, a Divine plan, or a defined destiny. If you do not share this belief, for the purposes of this workbook, please put your analytical mind to the side for a moment. Consider the possibility that you have a Life Purpose and that this Purpose has been predetermined in some way. I understand that for some, religious or spiritual beliefs aren't part of your day-to-day life and asking for this consideration may be out of your comfort zone. Personally, I wasn't brought up particularly religious and, although I suppose I had some concept of a Supreme Being or God, I didn't give it much thought. But together, let's put any doubts aside and use the tools I'll be discussing to discover our Life Purpose.

Oftentimes the impetus for us to wake up and make a decision to start living our Life Purpose comes when we are going through a life crisis. My awakening was maybe more dramatic than most. At forty, I thought I was quite happy with my life as a successful businesswoman. Then my life took a 180-degree turn—I was suddenly able to talk to dead people and do other freaky stuff! As you can imagine, this changed my life dramatically and soon after, I put my business endeavors aside and became a full-time medium.

Some people may think that being psychic or a medium is somehow ungodly or anti-Christian. Actually, becoming a medium was when I became aware of my Life Purpose. The existence of Divine guidance was shown to me and the big picture suddenly became clearer. This was when I started experiencing what I would call God. That being said, I am certainly not religious in an organized religion sense, but through my experiences as a medium, I have no doubt that there is an afterlife and a Divine presence. I believe in the existence of a benevolent energy, our creator, Divine Source. I have also seen, through my own and my client's experiences, that we do have past lives and that we go from life to life, learning and working on different themes.

If you have a hard time with this "woo-woo" spiritual stuff, at least consider the concept that your True Purpose is somehow a part of you that has been there from birth; it is part of your cell memory and your genetic makeup. When I talk about being in touch with the spirit world and receiving messages, simply consider this to be your intuition. When I talk about listening to your guides, think about listening to that inner you, your subconscious. And when I say talk to your guides, think about talking to your Higher Self, that part of you that seems to know more than the physical you. After all, it's all really the same thing….

Our Purpose Begins

In some cultures past lives are a part of the belief system. In our culture it is a notion that does not have widespread acceptance. Perhaps you believe in them or perhaps you do not. However, humor me for a moment. Imagine that we experience life after life and in between these lives, we go to a place we'll call Heaven. In this place we review what we've accomplished and what we didn't quite comprehend. We will look back at our shining moments and those we'd rather sweep under the carpet. Perhaps you will say to yourself, "I really would like another crack at that; I didn't quite get it last time" or "Boy, I would really like to experience [fill in the blank]." It is here in Heaven that we decide we'd like to have another go at the game of life. It's like a puzzle we've almost completed and have an urge to finish. So with this burning desire, we decide we're going to plunge back into life and have another physical existence.

Our soul friends in spirit may think we are very adventurous and perhaps say, "Good luck. I'll stay back here and watch." This will be our team on the other side, watching and rooting for us from the sidelines as we are the brave ones willing to experience life again. Our team in the spirit world will occasionally be able to pass a little guidance through our intuition, but mostly they are just there to love and support us.

In Heaven we decide how we might complete our unfinished business in our next life. Are there different routes we should take? Do we need some new tools to help us? We may have been working on the same issue through multiple lifetimes and are now determined to complete what we started. Perhaps there are some unfamiliar or interesting things we would like to experience that we haven't touched upon yet.

We choose things not because we know they would be pleasant but to experience all sides of life. To be well rounded in our soul's experience, we desire to learn, feel, and know all that life has to offer. We set up our major life events and select the theme or driving force of our life. As we choose from the buffet of life, we might say things like:

> *"I'd like to experience being a good parent and having a loving relationship with my children, but perhaps I should learn self-love as well because I didn't really comprehend it last time. So let's throw in some crappy relationships through which I can really learn to love myself."*
>
> *"I love music. This time I would like to have musical talent and experience joy through music. But a little financial stress might be good as well. I was a great businessman in my last life, so I now want to experience the opposite. Being a struggling musician, having passion but no resources, this should be a fun challenge!"*
>
> *"I would like to try not always being the one in control. I wonder what it feels like to have other people take care of me. Perhaps I could have a major health issue. I'll choose something quite difficult and then I can use what I learn to help others who are ill and, through this, express compassion."*

Thus we decide on our major themes, be it good or bad, pleasant or unpleasant. The more we take on and the more difficult the puzzle, the faster our soul growth will be. Perhaps in Heaven with all that bliss in the air, we are a bit overly enthusiastic and take on a little more than we realize. After all, if you were at level 19 on Angry Birds, would you really want to start at level 5 again? And so we set ourselves up with themes and tasks at the level that we think we can handle.

At this point you may be having thoughts like, "OMG what did I do? What was I thinking?" Don't worry; you can handle it.

We choose the people that we will meet, including our co-workers and friends. We also choose our family and our parents. WHAT?! Rewind! I chose my parents?!!! Oh yes, you absolutely did! We pick our relationships, including the wonderful people in our lives, and the unpleasant ones as well (this especially). You picked that jerk of a husband, your crummy sister, and even your mother-in-law! In fact, these are some of the closest, most beautiful souls you know. They wouldn't be able to affect you so deeply or impact you so much if you didn't really love them on a soul level. By the time we are born, we have already chosen our primary themes and many of the main players. Then a veil of amnesia comes over us and there is no going back.

No matter what major events we have chosen or what specific experiences we have agreed to, there is a direction and theme woven throughout our life. We have agreed to learn certain lessons. Along with this is an underlying Purpose that becomes apparent. This is our True Purpose or destiny and our very reason for being here.

So it is in Heaven that we decide our True Purpose, the theme that will dominate our experience throughout this lifetime–the vibration through which we will express our individuality, serve others, and advance spiritually. The Purpose that we choose may follow us through several lifetimes. We may be continuing where we left off in our previous life or perhaps we will continue this Purpose in our future lives.

We may call it True Purpose, Soul Purpose, True Calling, Destiny, Divine Purpose, our Life's Mission, our Life's Journey, or our Life's Path, but this is the theme that we experience throughout our life. For some, the word "destiny" gives the impression that it is something chosen for us, that we have no control over it, which can have a negative connotation. For example, a person might say it is their destiny to lose everything or to be alone and that there is nothing they can do to change it. Fatalism is not what our lives are about. For this reason, I prefer the term Soul Purpose. However, some of you may find the term a bit too New-Agey, so let's call it "True Purpose" or just "Purpose."

I want to emphasize the point that it is not anyone's destiny to be poor, lose everything, or anything else of that ilk. We haven't chosen a life path to experience pain or misery. No matter how bad things may seem, it is not our Purpose to live in poverty and struggle. Yes, we may have chosen a poverty-stricken upbringing or a period of financial strife, but this is not the be all and end all. We may have chosen financial issues that we can ultimately learn from. Perhaps we've chosen to learn that we can have a great life and be happy without having large amounts of money. Perhaps we want to understand how to manifest money or to learn to appreciate money but not to stay in a state of financial struggle forever. Similarly, we do not choose a True Purpose of to be in pain. Perhaps we can learn to endure pain, fight a disease, and then help others with similar conditions to cope and to heal. Our Purpose may be to get through a challenging circumstance, overcome misfortune, or to be valiant over a negative condition. It is never simply to experience something terrible and that's it!

Our path is not always smooth. There will be periods where we feel in sync with our life's journey and positive about our life. Then there will be times that we feel a bit lost, as we drift or take a side route. But when we are right there, when we are living our Purpose, we feel vibrant, happy, and in touch with the Divine. This is when we know we are living our True Purpose.

FREE WILL

We predetermine our major events and life moments along our theme. However, within this we do have free will. This is very important to know, so I will say it again:

We Have Free Will

Although we've set up the experiences that we will have, how we go about receiving those experiences is not set in stone. There is more than one way to achieve the same result. Many different paths lead to the same outcome and our path may wind around and around until it comes to its destination. It is the vibration, the experience of the energy that we have chosen.

I'll rephrase this a little bit differently. It is a feeling, a sensation, a knowing, an energetic vibration that we are seeking to experience. It is not a particular event that we want to experience, but rather a certain energy, and how exactly we get there doesn't really matter. For example, we may start out experiencing a feeling through a parent and then later continue this "lesson" through a romantic partner. Then we may think we've learned the lesson and moved on from the relationship only to experience this same theme once again with a co-worker. Can you think of themes or "feelings" you've had with a parent that you continued through a romantic partner or other significant person?

We choose life moments, experiences, and events that in some way are a reflection of our overall theme. These moments are mostly in sync with our

Purpose. However, they could also be in conflict to show us all sides of our Purpose so we can fully experience it. These moments could appear to challenge or go against our True Purpose through which we can find the determination to strengthen our direction.

We learn best through experience, not by someone else showing or telling us; we need to experience it ourselves. As we go through life and express our True Purpose, how we live our day-to-day moments are our choice. We have the free will to change our predetermined experiences. Even the major life challenges that we set for ourselves prior to birth can be changed or can play out in a different way. Perhaps shifting a major incident such as a difficult illness or stressful time may take more faith, more commitment, but it is always possible to do because we have free will.

To illustrate, I'll share the story of a man who came to one of my events. When I tuned into his energy, I was directed to work on his eyes. I actually had a vision of him being inside a very dark cave. I was seeing a past life where he'd been locked away in a deep, dark place purposely devoid of sunlight. My guides told me that he had brought that experience into this lifetime. In this past life there was a feeling of being unable to interact with life in a visual manner (to express vision was the term that came to me) and to continue that feeling, he'd set up a lesson to experience blindness in this lifetime.

As he stood in front of me, his eyes appeared to be perfectly normal. Then the message came that although he had set this experience for himself, it never needed to manifest fully because he had worked very hard in other areas of his life and, on a deep soul level, he no longer felt he needed to experience this loss of vision.

I asked if he had any problems with his eyes, and he replied that when he was younger, he had experienced many problems with his eyes. He had suffered from a condition where a cloudy sheath would grow over both his eyes, and every few years, it would need to be removed. However, it had recently lessened. Somehow he had "grown out of it," having had very few problems the last two years.

I then asked if he was working with young people in any capacity. It turned out that he coached sports at a high school! My guides explained to me that he had replayed his need to be able to express vision through helping these youths to see their way. In fact, he wasn't just an athletic coach; he counseled them in other areas as well. He'd actually dedicated his life to youths in need and had started a Big Brother type of program. Many times he'd helped them to get away from dangerous situations, literally allowing them to "see" a better life.

His eyes had shown great improvement in the last two years, which, not surprisingly, is the exact length of time that the youth program he helped to launch had been running. I shared what I had seen about the cave. Incredibly, it turned out that he'd had recurring nightmares of being blind and hates caves and dark places.

This example illustrates how, through our actions and free will, our lessons can play out in alternate ways. This man had, before birth, set up an experience, an energy/feeling that he felt he needed to complete. However, he found other ways in life to experience, learn, and express this energy, so he no longer needed to have the original "experience" of blindness.

I used to read Tarot cards and came to realize that what I was doing was simply reading a person's energy. I was tapping into their energy at that specific moment in time and was able to tell them what events were in their immediate future. This is because our reality is made up of our thoughts. Everything we are experiencing right now in our life is the result of our past thoughts and feelings. What we expect, what we dwell on, and what we speak of, create our reality. These thoughts and words sit in our energy field, and a psychic can sometimes pick up on them.

Ultimately, I realized that there isn't much of a point in having a psychic tell you what your future is. Your future is what you are setting up right now. If you don't like your options, simply change your way of thinking. This is what will shift your reality and create your new future. For me, there was no point in telling someone their future was in the cards because what I was seeing was simply their old thoughts. The better solution is to direct them to clarify what they want to happen, and then create the thoughts needed to bring this about.

What I did discover through giving readings is that for most people, a tarot reading was pretty accurate for about six months. This is because most people don't change their thinking very often. After about six months of thinking new thoughts and expressing your free will, the future is more likely to change and it's harder to predict accurately. My point is that the future changes because we have free will. We can change our direction to make our future into whatever we want. We have the free will to change everything for the positive and into wonderful experiences right now!!! So if you go for a reading and you don't like what is in your future, simply change your thoughts and direct them toward what you do want.

Our will is the strongest driving force we have. We are given the gift to make choices, though sometimes it feels like a curse when we make bad ones. However, we can choose anything–there is nothing we cannot change! It is like we have chosen our canvas and paint, and we know what kind of painting we want to create, but how we paint it, the brush strokes and the colors, are entirely up to us.

Health and Exit Points

I believe that we actually choose exit points at which time we may leave this life and "die." However, I also believe that even if we have chosen an illness as an exit point, we have the free will to change this. For instance, if we are battling an "incurable" disease and it is our time to go, we can actually, with strong determination, tell our soul that we have decided to stay a while longer. If we would like more experiences in this lifetime, and we have a reason to live, with tremendous inner strength, we can convince our own spirit to alter that exit point. We may also convince our soul that we need to stay longer for our True Purpose.

If someone develops a potentially fatal disease, it may be that they have chosen this illness through which they will exit. It could also be that they have chosen a health crisis through which they will find strength, overcome the odds, and be cured. Perhaps your True Purpose is going to be helping people through a similar illness. In this case you needed to experience this illness in order to follow your True Purpose, as you simply couldn't fulfill it properly without having lived it yourself. How do you know if you have chosen an illness as an exit point or to survive it? You don't! And you're not supposed to. You are supposed to fight like hell to the end.

What about children? Why would a child choose to have a difficult illness and pass away at an early age? This is a most heart wrenching and difficult question to comprehend. I believe that both the child and the parent agreed to it. Children who do this are truly little angels who have agreed to have a short lifespan in order to help another person's growth. For the parent to deal with the grief, pain, and sometimes guilt, is an extraordinarily difficult challenge. The parent and the child have both set up this experience and, on a soul level, they have the ability and the free will to change the outcome. Keep telling the Universe that you need to be here together for a very long time and describe the Purpose you will have together.

Some of you may have gone through excruciating experiences, and it is very difficult to comprehend that in some way, you chose this. No matter what it was, in some way, your soul experienced growth. If you can look at it in this way and know that you did grow, perhaps this will help to lessen the pain. There is nothing that is simply pointless or cruel. Nothing is an accident.

KARMA, THEMES, AND PREDETERMINED ASPECTS

Karma

As I say the word Karma, I know you are groaning. It's not all bad. Karma is anything we have brought into our lives that originated before our present incarnation. So, yes, our True Purpose is our part of our karma. Our True Purpose is the theme for our life and probably has been for many lifetimes. It was set up before this life, so it is karmic in nature.

The term karma is most often used in relation to specific experiences or relationships. These could be unfinished "feelings" that our soul still yearns to work through, which came from a previous lifetime. It could be karmic that we find ourselves accused of a crime that we never committed or were unfairly treated by our peers. It could be karmic that we find ourselves scared of heights or having other phobias from a previous life experience. It could be karmic that we feel controlled or repressed as this was our expression in a previous lifetime as a slave or a victim and we never completed that lesson.

We also can have specific karma with people. In a family one child may be favored, and the other child always gets the raw end of the deal. In situations where this is karmic, it usually appears to a bystander that there is no apparent reason for it. The parent often is not even aware of anything they are doing.

Most of our relationships are karmic, including our lovers, our family, and our bosses. Some may have deeper meaning than others but most of them, even passing acquaintances, we have known in some way before. After all, we reincarnate in soul groups, often waiting for us all to be together so we can reincarnate at the same time.

Our romantic relationships are usually karmic, meaning we had an experience with this person in a past life, and we are either continuing the same pattern or perhaps have chosen to reverse our roles and experience another side of ourselves. So meeting a "soul mate" means to meet a person we have known before and wish to further explore our spiritual relationship. This could be a wonderful meeting of two people who have a loving connection and experience deep, unconditional love. However, a soul mate can also be someone you know and love from before who is about to teach you some very unpleasant lessons. After all, who better to push your buttons and affect you profoundly and intensely, than a soul mate that you love deeply.

Karma can also be physical in nature. Sometimes we bring physical issues or ailments as a result of something in the past that we feel is unfinished. You may even see people with a birthmark that was a scar from a wound in a previous life.

I had a friend who had continual problems with his lower left leg. The problems were originally caused by a teenage accident that crushed his ankle. Other issues and complications arose as an adult, all due to this initial accident. But is that where it actually originated?

We did a past life regression. He found himself in a previous life during World War II. He was in the midst of a horribly gruesome battle. The last thing he remembered was taking a step, hearing a horrific noise, being propelled up, and flying through the air. At that moment he realized that he had stood on a landmine. His lower left leg was blown completely off, leaving him numb from the knee down. The last thing he remembered was being carried away on a stretcher and looking down to see his lower left leg missing.

Through this regression we discovered that his teenage injury, which had caused so many leg issues in this lifetime, was not a random "accident" but rather it had been predetermined to manifest in some manner in this life. It was the continuation of an energy or a feeling from a previous lifetime which he felt had been left unresolved. Much of the basis of spiritual healing is to use such discoveries and then dissolve the initial cause, which can bring great healing.

We tend to think of karma as a negative or bad thing and look at it as an obstacle or difficulty that has come from the past to haunt us. People often see it as some nasty "lesson" from God. This is simply not true. God does not set obstacles in our way or throw us into difficult and painful situations. It just doesn't make sense that God, this beautiful energy that is made of unconditional love, would want to thrust us into nasty, hurtful experiences. God supports us and loves us but gives us free will. We are the ones who set up difficult and unpleasant situations because we want to experience all sides of our soul. So it is a longing that we have to experience life and all it has to offer.

If we set ourselves an experience or lesson and we didn't complete it or fully experience what it had to offer in a past life, we then have the desire to finish what we started. We have a compulsion to follow-through and experience the issue. We would not feel like we accomplished much if we just sat back and allowed God to bring us only beautiful experiences. We need to feel like we worked for it, that we completed the puzzle ourselves. Opening the newspaper to the crossword puzzle and finding it already filled in would not be much fun. Still, when we become consciously aware of our True Purpose and our karmic "tests," there are ways we can progress through them more quickly and easily.

Karma playing out can also feel good; we just tend to dwell on the difficult situations. Karma can present us with the opportunity for a beautiful and joyous vacation. It can help us to receive recognition and acclaim for our accomplishments. The perfect home and a loving relationship can be the result of karma. Karma plays though our life in our beautiful moments as well.

We often wonder about karma and how it works when we cross over. You may have heard about people who have been to the other side (usually through a near-death experience) and then come back. These people may talk about a "life review," where upon crossing to the other side, your life flashes before you. It is true that when you cross to the other side, you will look back on what you have accomplished. You'll surely look at your True Purpose in life and contemplate the areas where you did a good job and where you fell short. You actually review and experience the good things you did and where you weren't so good. You "feel" the feelings that you imparted on others when you did something nice for them. You also "feel" the feelings that you caused when you did something not so nice to someone. So you actually feel the pain, hurt, guilt, and other feelings that you inflicted on someone else. This is not God punishing you; this is simply your soul more clearly understanding your journey.

If you inflicted pain on others, you often will want to feel the reverse in your next life (as part of your learning and growth) and those people are going to come back with you. The good news is you don't have to wait until you die, you can work on it right now. You can make a conscious effort to give back in areas where you know you have hurt others. Even if you can't make amends with that particular person, you can "pay back" your karma by helping others in a similar way. Take an honest review of your life and think about the people you may have hurt. Then think about how you could treat others differently, even if they are not the person who's been hurt. How can you give back and make up for any pain or hurt you have inflicted on others? It is far easier to alter your life and work though things that you have done wrong now, in this lifetime. Otherwise that person is going to blindside you in your next life and you're going to say, "Why did I deserve that?" or "I didn't do anything to them…!" It makes you look at things differently, doesn't it?

So karma can relate to our theme and True Purpose, but it can also relate to the experiences that originated in another lifetime. It can refer to certain events or relationships and the energy we create through them as well. Each of these experiences are, of course, beautifully interwoven seamlessly into our theme and True Purpose. They are individual experiences of expressions of our soul journey.

Multiple Themes

Although we have chosen one main True Purpose, we may have several themes that make up that purpose. We may also have lesser themes, which give us the opportunity to test our faith or through which we can find clarity. Sometimes these themes work in harmony, such as a main theme of "helping disabled people receive love and care" and a secondary theme of "providing healing to others through the spoken word." As you can see, these work beautifully together. In other cases our themes may be in conflict, such as one requiring the person to be in the spotlight or in the public eye, and another theme requiring them to be introverted, spending significant time alone in reflection. Michael Jackson and Princess Diana come to mind as celebrity examples of those who may have had conflicting Life Purposes.

I am often asked if a person's True Purpose can be completed and another one started in the same lifetime. In other words, can our True Purpose change during our life? This, although possible, is very unlikely. If we experience a major shift in our personality or in what drives us, it could be that our spirit guides are changing. Perhaps we are suddenly becoming more in sync with our Life Purpose, which wasn't so clear before. It could be that we have matured in our consciousness and are feeling our True Purpose for the very first time. Maybe we are dealing with a significant karmic event that is teaching us through conflict or distracting us at the moment.

Sometimes it can be difficult to tell what is part of our True Purpose and what is some other piece of karma that has come along and is not particularly a part of our path. Although we have our main drive or True Purpose, we are thrown additional opportunities for spiritual growth, helping others, and opening our awareness.

There are also times when we want to change our True Purpose. Just as there are times when trying to solve a puzzle or when trying to achieve a goal that you may feel like giving in and calling it quits. Sometimes we feel like throwing in the towel on our Purpose as well. These are usually during challenging times of blockages and tests we have given ourselves. If we can be clear on our Purpose, it helps us to persevere and to get through these blocks. Of course, when we do, we often deserve and feel a spiritual growth spurt.

Divinely Orchestrated

There are no accidents. You choose the perfect family, the perfect environment to set up the conditions for the experiences you wish to have. This is a concept that many take issue with. Those of you who've faced a serious disease may say that you did not choose this illness but that it is in your ancestry or your genetic makeup and that is why you developed it. Yes, that may be true, but you also set your genetic makeup to fit the experience that you are choosing to have, not the other way around.

What if an accident caused your health problems or a doctor's mistake resulted in your poor health? You might believe that an uncle who beat you as a child caused a cascade of emotional issues that dictated the direction of your life. All of these may be true, but the point is that life sets things up to create the perfect environment for what we wish to experience and to accomplish in our lifetime.

As I've discussed, we choose the family that we are born into as well. The energy of our family tree and our ancestors are a component of our energetic makeup. We actually carry the energy of thoughts and feelings that are passed down through our DNA from our ancestral line. For example, you may carry feelings of guilt or a fear of relationships but not recall having had an experience that this stems from. Perhaps, in fact, these feelings came from a great grandmother who had an affair. The energy of guilt was then passed down through the genetic line and is an energy carried by you from birth. In this circumstance you may have no understanding of where these feelings and this energy came from. Yet it is part of your energy field and part of your individuality.

Others believe that our lives are preordained by things like astrology or numerology. These people may say that our personality, career, our whole life is laid out accurately in our astrological chart. But remember, you choose the perfect chart for the experiences (and difficulties) that you are going to have. The same is true for palm reading, numerology, and the like. Yes, they are all perfectly designed by you prior to birth. We also have the free will to change them as well as we evolve on our path.

So now we know that we've chosen our parents and are born into a family whose circumstances are right for our Purpose. We have the "perfect" environment (good or bad) to experience the life events that we have predetermined. But then how does this fit in with the path of our family members? Our parents surely have their own True Purpose and major life events, so how could their events link up with ours?

This is one of the great mysteries of life. It is difficult to comprehend how many different parts need to be lined up exactly. Each person that is going to be a significant player in your life has been brought to you in perfect sync. Your experiences are going to mesh together so that you receive what you need and they receive what they need. You each will have the perfect astrology chart for this complementary experience. In numerology, your names and birth numbers will have the vibration to match exactly the life experiences you will have. The same is true for the lines on your hands (palmistry) and the reading of your eyes (oculomancy)! Our extended families are also in sync. How could it be that we all match up at the same time? It seems to be an impossibility, but this is what happens.

Then throw in free will. We have the free will to change an event. Yes, we have set up certain occurrences in our lives, but once in the game of life, if we decide we have absorbed enough of a particular experience, perhaps we don't need to go on to a second or third experience of the same vibration. Or we may choose to learn something through one person and then decide to move on to another for that same lesson. How can all this stay in sync with what the other people have chosen and their own free will as well? Somehow it does. I believe the answer is not something that our human mind is capable of fully understanding at this time. Just know that it works perfectly.

Predestined Family

The notion that we have a predestined family is a hard one for many to swallow. How could we have chosen such an abusive dad or an unloving mother? Our parents and close family are going to be the major players in our life and almost always they will have a strong karmic tie. This doesn't mean that it's a bad or hard relationship; it could be a wonderful connection. Our family members are probably going to be the most important of our journey.

How we are brought up, the environment we are born into, and whether we are privileged or poor, is also going to be a part of our journey that has been carefully chosen by us. This includes our nationality, culture, our parent's jobs, etc. which all bring a vibration for us to experience. It is all perfectly interwoven for our perfect life experience.

To illustrate, I'll use my own family history. When I was seven years old, my father suffered a massive heart attack and died. He was only 43 years old. My mother was left to raise two small children, with no insurance to help, and she was completely unprepared for this major life event. My mother made the best of it. She chose never to remarry, worked two jobs, and was able to raise my brother and I without much want for anything.

Did I choose this circumstance? I am sure I did. We choose our parents, and I obviously chose to have that experience. My mother, my brother, and even my father all chose this as well. Of course my father didn't consciously know. It was a surprise to everyone. But on a soul level, he knew. I am sure my mother learned from this experience as part of her journey. Perhaps her lesson was to be stronger and more independent. Perhaps this was one of the themes she wanted to experience. This major life event affected the direction of all of our lives.

Now for the really strange part of the story. My dad had been my mom's only real love, but prior to meeting him, she'd briefly dated another man who was named John. John had been madly in love with her, and my mom occasionally wondered how her life would have played out if she had married him instead. Well, years later, my mom was in England and happened to bump into John's sister. My mom asked how John was doing. His sister shared the sad news that John had passed away quite young. At 43 he'd had a sudden, massive heart attack and died!

Yes, John was the same age as my dad when he, too, died of a massive heart attack! So, my mom would have gone through the same exact experience had she married John! So what does this mean? Perhaps my mom, myself, and the rest of our family had chosen this life event. How exactly did that happen? Whether my mom had chosen my dad or John, was free will playing out? Yes, small things in our lives would have been different, but the major life event would have been the same. So did my mom attract men into her life that had also set this life plan? Yes, absolutely!

As you can see, we may have set up a predestined life event, but exactly how we go about experiencing this event and with whom is our choice as we have free will. When I was marrying for the second time, some of my friends told me I was marrying a man who was exactly the same as my ex-husband. I couldn't believe that. He looked nothing like him and acted completely different. But years later, I could see that I was back having those same learning lessons that I thought I'd skipped out of when I ended my first marriage. I had free will to change the circumstances, but my soul had brought me back to the same experiences once again. Luckily, at some point we can wake up and say, "I learned from that experience; I understand and have assimilated the wisdom gleaned from that experience, and I don't need to have it anymore."

When your mom doesn't like your boyfriend or your sister doesn't like your girlfriend, you may want to think twice. Other people can stand back and see our life from another perspective. They can assess the strategy of the war, while we are in the midst of the battle and can't see a darn thing around us. This is not to say that we should always listen to these friends and family members. Perhaps our lesson is to stand up for ourselves and not be influenced by those around us. But we should listen to what they have to say, as their perspective may be less clouded than our own.

The family we have in our life and our close relationships are all meant to be. Even if life takes a few strange turns to get us there, this does not mean it is random or an accident. Where we are is where we are meant to be; whoever is around us, is who is meant to be around us.

To illustrate this point, once again I'll use an example from my own family. I have a cousin Ric in England who is very spiritual, and I love him dearly. We have a deep connection where we feel like we know and understand each other in a beautiful, loving way. He is definitely one of my more pleasant soul mates. His mom, Pauline-Mary, is my Auntie Pauline whom I dearly love as well. Ric wasn't born into the family; he was adopted. My Auntie Pauline thought she couldn't have children, but as soon as Ric was adopted and officially home, Pauline realized she was pregnant with Ric's brother.

Although Ric loves his mom very much, at the legal age of 18 he decided that he would like to meet his birth mother, just out of curiosity. So Ric went through the legal paperwork and was able to track down and meet his birth mother. Not surprisingly, she had been a young teen, only sixteen years old, when she had become pregnant and was forced to give him up. However, there was a little bit of confusion at the adoption agency while setting up the meeting. You see, to his and their surprise, his birth mother's name was also Pauline-Mary!

Now Pauline-Mary is not such a common name in England, so what are the odds of that? The adoption agency staff must have had a real chuckle that day. And the parallels in their names don't end there! His mom and his birth mother both have maiden names that begin with "M" and both of their married names begin with "L."

So is this a case where the Universe screwed up? Was there a little blip where Ric was supposed to be born to my Auntie Pauline and they got the right name but the wrong person? We have no idea. It seems kind of odd, but there are no such things as coincidence. What it means, I don't know. But he is with the correct soul family now; he is where he's meant to be.

It is almost incomprehensible when you think of all the players in your life and how your major events and themes could sync up with theirs so perfectly, but they do.

Multiple Dimensions

We live in a multi-dimensional Universe. So while we imagine that there is only one of us living our True Purpose, there are actually multiple versions of us in many different dimensions. They are also perfectly coordinated together. We can even move from one dimension to another without realizing we are doing it! Perhaps you have an ailment and suddenly it disappears. One possibility is that your soul decided that you no longer needed this experience, and you merged with another version of yourself. You align with the image of yourself where that ailment did not exist and merged it into this reality to bring your body into perfect health.

I believe that when we want to manifest something into our life, it is right there and available to us, perhaps in another dimension just a nanosecond of time away. It is possible, in fact, to bring one dimension into another. There is also no such thing as time. Time is an illusion. There is no past or future, only now.

All this is food for thought, but before we go too far in depth, let's concentrate on understanding our True Purpose in the dimension and experience we are living right now, at this moment.

The Waking Age

Often we get closer to our Life Purpose later in life, as we become older and hopefully wiser. Some people talk about having a midlife crisis or refer to the second half of their life. When people reach a certain age, which for many it is around forty, we suddenly have a different outlook on life. Often this is the turning point at which we realize our True Purpose, whether it is consciously or unconsciously.

During the first half of our lives, we are usually busy collecting the experiences that will help us. We are still developing the skill sets and tools of life. We are trying on various careers and testing our likes and dislikes to discover what truly makes us tick. Normally it is after this time spent in discovery that our True Purpose becomes more in focus.

Actually, we live very close to our True Purpose when we are young children, but then we start to put that behind us as our soul memory lessens and we get into the game of life. However, at a certain point in our life, we come to a place where our soul knows our Purpose and it is time to actively get on that path.

DEFINING YOUR TRUE PURPOSE

Why Know Your True Purpose?

Defining our main True Purpose, as well as other lesser themes and karmic lessons, enables us to see our life more clearly. Then we can more consciously direct our thoughts and activities to our True Purpose. Why does it help us to know our Life's Purpose? After all, if it is predetermined, and we are stuck with what we chose, know it or not, what difference does it make?

When we are on our soul's journey is when we feel completely connected. It not only brings us happiness and a sense of satisfaction, but on a much deeper soul level, we are overjoyed. When we consciously understand our True Purpose, we can actively get there much faster. We can direct our efforts to experiences that are more in sync with our Purpose. We can consciously choose experiences that we know will "feel" right. It helps us not to be so affected by the obstacles in our life because we can see their purpose and move on. We understand our underlying mission and can now make a conscious effort to get there.

When you have a clearer picture of what you are striving for, it is easier to stand back and view your life. You will start to see certain events that you have manifested and the reasons why they've come to you. You will see your relationships more clearly and why their dynamics are the way they are. This enables you to more quickly process the information, feel the experiences, and release them. When we can see the big picture, the smaller pieces don't seem so bad.

The more quickly we can recognize the lessons we've set up for ourselves, the more we can find the joy in life. Our purpose here is not to experience one nasty lesson after another. Our purpose here is to find joy in our lives. Our purpose is to experience love. Yes, perhaps we have to go through much to get there; but the game of life is to experience this love, this joy, this happiness, and to feel this beauty in our lives.

Being off-track brings us a feeling of boredom, depression, hopelessness, and a feeling of being "lost." In fact, when we lose our way, we can become so depressed that we may even want to give up on life and return to Heaven. We can actually create illnesses in our physical body from a spiral of negative energy.

Our whole purpose is to get closer and closer to that wonderful feeling where we feel fulfilled, with purpose, and it brings us immense joy. Though no one can be living their True Purpose one hundred percent of the time. Being on our True Purpose comes in spurts, little moments, and meaningful events in our lives. What we strive for is to understand our True Purpose, to really connect with that purpose, so that we can experience more moments in our life of this true connection.

No Competition

I noticed that when some of my students would first start to think about their True Purpose, their mission and their talents in life, they'd believe that we would all want to do the same thing. They thought that we'd all want the best and therefore would be in competition with each other. First of all, everyone does not want the same thing. There are people who want to be leaders and pioneers, craving the public eye. Then there are others who truly love to be behind the scenes and be the organizer or supporter of another. Some love to be creative, spontaneous, and directed by their intuition. There are even those who actually love to solve math problems all day!

Even within the same field, we may have different desires. In fact, as you discover your Life Purpose, you will see that each person is entirely different. When we know our True Purpose, we no longer feel in competition with others, but rather we can see how we complement each other. When we're on our True Purpose, we realize that we are not taking away from another. Nor is there any lack of jobs, roles, or whatever we need for our True Purpose. We can recognize that others have not "taken" it already. There is a plentiful supply, as that supply is Divine Source. Our True Purpose originates from the Divine so, of course, everything we need to fulfill it is easily within our reach.

The Process of Discovering

Some information about your True Purpose can be garnered through asking another to help guide you or analyze your life. You can even tune in psychically and talk to your spirit guides. Although this is helpful, it is important that you are actively involved in this journey of discovery. To be told your True Purpose or simply to know it is not the same as "feeling" your True Purpose, for only you can resonate with your True Purpose. Only you "know" your life path when you are connected to it.

I know some of you will be disappointed as you were hoping I was just going to tell you what your True Purpose is. Don't be, you are now going to discover it for yourself. If I were to just tell you your True Purpose, it wouldn't have the same effect. You wouldn't really get it and feel it deeply if I just told you. Do you have children? Have you tried telling them not to do something because you have tried it and it turned out badly? And do they listen or do they do it anyway? You see, we have to experience things for ourselves. It's just not the same to be told that the stove is hot and it burns. We have to stick our finger on it and try it for ourselves anyway!

Besides, the fun of being on a journey is the journey itself. When you reach your destination, the journey is over. It's not about arriving, it's how you get there and all the fun stuff along the way that counts. It is through soul-searching and feeling this connection that you will be able to direct your life in order to be on your path more of the time.

The Influence of Others

As you go through the discovery of your True Purpose, you are going to make sure that these are your own wants and desires. Often we do something to make others happy. Many of you may have been influenced by your parents and did what they wanted you to do. Sometimes we build our whole career or our whole life on what we think others want us to do or to make someone else proud of us. As you go through these exercises, make sure you are searching and truthfully asking about what *you* want. Please answer honestly and without self-judgment.

PART II
FINDING YOUR TRUE PURPOSE

We are now going to go through the process of analyzing your life and discovering the hidden signs that will help you to define your True Purpose. This will be used to formulate your True Purpose into a statement that resonates with you. Note—It is not the final statement that is important, but rather it is through the process of discovery that you will find yourself again….

FEELING YOUR TRUE PURPOSE

What does it feel like when you are on your life path? You instinctively know this. There have been times in your life where things seem to work perfectly, everything is great, and life just seems to flow seamlessly. Even if this has only happened for a few fleeting moments, we've all had occasions where life felt wonderful.

Think about the moments in your life when you felt you were living your True Purpose. You may want to consider:

- The times you achieved something great.
- The highlights of your life.
- Times when you triumphed over a personal difficulty.

- Occasions when you received recognition for something that you are proud of.
- Periods where you felt like life flowed perfectly because you were connected and living your True Purpose.

Think of words or phrases that describe those feelings. The following are some examples:

- Alive
- Energized
- Bursting with happiness
- Full of joy
- Enlightened
- Elated
- Overwhelmed with tears of happiness
- Grateful
- Fulfilled

- At ease
- Peaceful
- Content
- Appreciated
- Feeling connected to a Higher Power/God
- A feeling of belonging
- A warm sensation in your heart
- A glow around you
- Deep love

Circle or mark the words that are meaningful to you and write down any additional words or phrases that you feel express this.

_____
_____
_____
_____
_____
_____
_____

Now close your eyes for a moment and remember those feelings of being in the flow, when life felt wonderful. This is what it feels like when you are living your True Purpose. To experience this to a greater extent is to be more connected and more Divinely guided. This is what you should be striving for. Yes, we choose obstacles and challenges to make life interesting, but when we overcome them and are on our path, this bliss is what life feels like. We are not meant to suffer throughout life. The more suffering we experience does not make us closer to the Divine; suffering is only something we, ourselves, have put in our path. We are meant to feel Divine connection with great joy and love in our life; this is the purpose of our life. Our purpose is to get to the point where we feel this more and more. This is what the Divine wants us to feel. This is true spiritual enlightenment.

Guidance from Heaven

As discussed previously, when we are born into our life we have a soul group, a team of supporters on the other side. They are friends, family members, and loved ones (and even those who were once enemies). We have known them from past lives, and they travel with us in soul groups. We also have one main spirit guide who is a highly evolved being that has been with us from the time of our birth.

Our main spirit guide is a higher Master spirit. Though our relatives may be around us for love and support, a passed away family member is not normally a spirit guide. Our main spirit guide is there as our partner to guide us through life. They know us intimately and know our True Purpose. They love us unconditionally and are, in fact, on the journey with us, just from the other side. They are here to guide us along our path. We can receive help from them if we just take the time to ask and look for the signs they are trying to give us.

Besides our main guide, other guides will come and go as we learn something new or go through another phase in our life. We also have talent guides. For example, if you are writing a book, an experienced author in spirit may help. If you are going through nursing school, a spirit doctor may be holding your hand. These spirits may come and go, and this is sometimes why we experience personality shifts. Our priorities and our likes and dislikes may change. It is not that we have changed our Purpose or direction, it is that our spirit guidance is changing.

A family member in spirit may be close to us. Others may remark that we have the personality of our grandfather, for instance. Perhaps you have a knack for fixing things just like he did. This is not because you are a reincarnation of this person (which although possible, is unlikely). It is because they are around and close to you. So, if they bring you a certain personality trait or talent, is this not your own talent? Yes, of course it is. Just as we receive talents through our experiences, our astrological chart, etc., our spirit guide influences are no different.

We can gain much from the spirits around us—our loved ones and our guides. In particular, we receive help from our main guide and our talent guides. Sometimes things just come to us. We may call this intuition. We may call it coincidence. But I believe it is heavenly guidance. The key to talking to our guides is through meditation. Connect through quiet reflection where we go inside ourselves and feel a deeper connection to the spirit world.

Ask Your Guides about Your True Purpose

Let's start by asking your spirit guides about your True Purpose. The following is a meditation to connect with your guides. You may talk to your main spirit guide and also connect with any other guides that are helping you. Perhaps there is a guide who has come in specifically because you are going through a particular period of your life and they can provide the tools to assist you. Often your guides have the knowledge that you will need or that will help you in the area of your life you are working on.

In this meditation you will be asking your guides to reveal their personality and the Life Tools they bring. (I will discuss Life Tools more fully in the next chapter. For now, just know that they are our talents, attributes, and personality traits that we need to carry out our True Purpose and they are given to us when we arrive in this life.) Your guide will present you with a box that will give insight into your gifts and True Purpose.

If you have a hard time believing in the concept of spirit guidance, consider it that you are talking to your subconscious. Go ahead with the exercise as if you are playing a visualization game with your subconscious or Higher Self. This should bring about the same result.

Meditation Preparation

Prepare – Find a place where you can meditate quietly without being disturbed. Sit comfortably (but not lying down where you might actually fall asleep). Light a white or a purple candle and place it in front of you.

Protect – Visualize a bright star in the sky and this star's white rays of light beaming down over the top of your head. Imagine this white healing light coming down over your shoulders, slowly down over your body, and completely enveloping your entire body in pure white energy in the highest of goodness. Then imagine tree roots of white light going from the soles of your feet down into Mother Earth. You are now protected in this bubble of white light energy where only good energies can come into your aura.

Breathing/Relaxation – Sitting comfortably, place your hands, palms upward, on your lap. Concentrate on your breathing, taking a deep breath in from your nose, holding it for a second, then exhaling long and forcefully through your mouth. With each breath in, concentrate on bringing in beautiful white light. With each breath out, envision releasing negative energy and relaxing deeper and deeper.

When you are ready for the meditation, you may begin. (You may want a friend to read this aloud to you or familiarize yourself first so that you don't need to read this during the meditation.)

Meet Your Guides and Discover Your True Purpose Meditation

Feel a column of white light coming down through your Crown Chakra, running through your body, opening and lighting up each of your chakras as the energy passes through. Then see the white light coming out from your feet and going down into Mother Earth, grounding you.

Now imagine that your angel is standing behind you, caressing you with their wings. Your angel is going to help you raise your vibrational energy. Leaving your physical body grounded, sense that your spiritual body is vibrating a little bit higher, a little bit faster, a little bit lighter. Imagine your angel helping you by gently lifting your spiritual body higher, up and out of your physical body. Imagine that you are floating into the sky, gently held and lifted by your angel.

As you float up into the sky, completely protected by white light, you see a door ahead of you in the clouds. It is an inviting door. Visualize what it looks like. When you are ready you can open the door and go inside.

Now you are inside your personal meditation room. This is your very own room up on the seventh plane. Decorate it however you like with your favorite furniture, your favorite art, your favorite colors, etc. Give it a beautiful window with a view. Perhaps it has a view of a waterfall or the ocean. Perhaps the window is open and a gentle breeze is flowing through.

Place a cozy couch in your room and go sit on it. Now ask your spirit guide to come in. Place your attention in front of you. You see a ball of mist coming towards you. You may not see your guide at first; you may just feel a loving presence. Just know that someone is in the mist and as they approach, the mist disappears and you can see them more clearly. This is one of your guides coming forward to greet you. Ask them to sit beside you. Feel their presence. Thank them from your heart. Feel the love they are giving you and send them back your appreciation.

If you cannot see your guide clearly, look down at their feet and notice what they are wearing. As you look up their body, see their clothing and get a sense of who they are. They may have been previously incarnated (lived on earth before). Try to get a sense of when that was. What kind of personality do you sense from them (e.g., serious, fun, loving, healing, wise)? Ask their hair color and their eye color. Ask if they can tell you their name. Feel the love they are sending and thank them for helping and working with you. Ask if they have a message about the Life Tools they are helping you with. Listen for an answer.

Now your guide offers you a gift. This is a message or gift to help reveal what you need to know about your True Purpose and what talents you are using or need. It could be presented as a box or a package. For instance, it may appear as a plain box, an ornate box, or some other kind of parcel. Accept this gift and when you are ready, you can open your box (or unwrap the package) and look inside. There may be an object or two within. There may be a note written to you. You may see a color or light. You may receive a feeling or a knowing. Perhaps your box is empty and that's ok too. Ask your guide what it means if you are not sure. Thank your guide for whatever you received, this wonderful gift, and if you are unsure of its meaning, ask that it be revealed to you later. Then put the lid back on and visualize taking the box or package into your heart.

What you receive may be a gift to help you on your True Purpose journey. It may be an insight that you need to know about your journey. You also have other guides and can ask for them to come forward. There are many beautiful energies that are working with you and are available to help you.

End by thanking your guides for being with you and say goodbye for now. Know that your guides remain close to you and that you can always come back to this special place to talk to them.

Now it is time to return to the physical world but know that this is a place to which you can always return. Imagine leaving this room and gently floating back to earth. As your spiritual body lowers, the energy becomes slightly heavier, slightly denser; your cells are vibrating slightly slower. Allow your body to gently float back down, still held and supported by your angel.

As you reach the earth, gently sink into your physical body. Feel your physical body. Be aware of your feet on the ground and your bottom in the chair. Wiggle your fingers. When you feel completely back in your physical body, slowly and gently open your eyes. You are now awake, refreshed, and ready to take on your life challenges, knowing that your guides are always with you.

What did you experience? What kind of a box or package did you receive? Did the contents of the box reveal anything about your True Purpose? Did it reveal a talent you have or a Life Tool? Did it reveal something that you needed to know? For example, if you saw a pen, it may be an indication that writing is a part of your True Purpose. A crystal wand may suggest involvement with natural healing modalities. The specific meaning of an object and its message will be unique to each person. Some of you may not have been able to visualize a gift but rather you saw a light or an energy. Perhaps you just had a feeling.

The box itself has meaning as well. For example, a plain, earthen box may mean that you work better and connect easier through nature and natural healing. Spending more time in nature could be beneficial. A box decorated with shells might reflect the ocean. Perhaps your Purpose is connected to water, the ocean, or marine life. A diamond box could indicate to bring a sense of glamour to what you do.

You may be given a message about a Life Tool or an indication of how to better connect with your guides. Your gift and even your guide's persona may reveal a connection between you (or your abilities) and them. For instance, if your guide looks like an Egyptian Pharaoh, you may understand why you have an affinity for pyramids or a desire to lead. Similarly, if your guide is a monk, you may better understand your desire to be of service to others.

During the meditation, did it feel like you were making it up? Communication with your guides often feels like your imagination. It's ok if it seems like you are just making up a story. You will learn from experience that it is not simply your imagination.

Were you able to visualize your guides? Don't be discouraged if you do not "see" a fully-formed person sitting next to you. Personally, I find that it is difficult to visualize my guides straight on. I have an easier time asking to see their profile or a specific feature, such as hair color or eye color. Some people cannot visualize anything at all. In this case, ask yourself, "Did I sense a loving energy? Did I see a color or light?" Your psychic senses develop over time and each time you do this meditation, a little more may be revealed to you.

Write down what you saw in your box, even if it doesn't make sense. Also note any insights or information that you received about your True Purpose or what you need for your journey.

_____

_____

_____

_____

_____

_____

_____

LIFE TOOLS

Finding Your Life Tools

All of the talents, attributes, and personality traits that we need to carry out our True Purpose are given to us when we arrive in this life. Let's collectively call these Life Tools. We wouldn't be expected to carry out our Life Purpose without having been given the necessary tools for the theme we have chosen. That would be like having a theme of "to bring joy to people through making them laugh" but having no talent for comedy. Life Tools may also be latent. We may have potential Life Tools that we need to develop or they need to be "discovered." They are there, though.

Life Tools that are talents may be obvious, such as being musically inclined or having a scientific mind, though some can be less discernable. However, don't think of Life Tools only as things like a talent for the arts, sports, or scientific pursuits. Many Life Tools can be difficult to identify or uncover. They can also come in hidden form. Some may even appear to be a negative trait at first. For example, someone who worries about every little thing may have the Life Tool of "an eye for detail."

We also have a tendency not to own our Life Tools. A person may say things like:
- I have a talent for something because I learned it from my father.
- I got a specific personality trait from my mother.
- I learned to be hard-working because I was born into a poor family, and it was necessary for my survival.
- I have a talent that came to me through my astrology chart.

Yes, these statements may be true. But remember, as determined before birth, we are born into the right situation where we will inherit or develop the Life Tools that we need.

We also come with all the Life Tools that we need to carry out our secondary and lesser Themes as well as the ones that we need to deal with karmic lessons. We may even be developing a Life Tool for a future life that we may never need to use in this lifetime.

Generally people will have about 3-6 main Life Tools that stand out and then a few secondary ones. Discovering the Life Tools that you use most will help you to discover your True Purpose. We will attempt to find all of our Life Tools, including the latent ones. We'll start by making a comprehensive list of all the possible Life Tools we think that we may have. Then we will see which ones stand out as the most important.

First think about the most obvious Life Tools you think you have. Think about your talents and attributes. What immediately comes to mind? This is not a time to be modest and you can keep this list to yourself if you are afraid of appearing too boastful. Write down any words that resonate with you. They can be an adjectives, adverbs, verbs, roles, personality traits, talents, or feelings that describes a Life Tool that you think you may have.

_____

_____

_____

We will now go through some exercises to clarify your Life Tools and find any "hidden" ones. Do not skip ahead in this section. Do not read the rest of the chapter. Do each exercise in order.

Your Life Tools List

Look over the list of Life Tool examples below. Any Life Tool that you already have on your own list (from the previous section), mark as one that jumped out immediately. If a Life Tool you previously identified is not on the list, write it in. Some Life Tools are roles, such as "manager," while others describe one's personality, like "brave." The type of word (e.g., noun, adjective, talent, feeling) doesn't matter; it is how you resonate with that word.

Now look over the following list and ask yourself, "Which words fit me?" Take a moment to contemplate each Life Tool example to see how it makes you *feel.* Which ones do you think you may be using or have the potential to use? (Don't be modest.) You don't need to hone in on the most important Tools just yet. Some on the list may be for your lesser themes or karmic work. It is fine to choose ten or twenty of these Life Tools. What is most important is their resonance, not the number you choose.

• •

* Note – You are going to be working on this list quite a bit as you go back and forth, adding more and then narrowing down your choices. Some Life Tools will become more prominent than others. You may want to either work in pencil or make photocopies of this list to use as a work in progress. You can then fill in these pages when your final choices are more complete.

• •

Part 2: Finding Your True Purpose

Life Tool List – In Progress

- Artistic (art)
- Artistic (other)
- Creative
- Imaginative
- Writer
- Musician or musically inclined
- Entrepreneurial
- Leader
- Manager
- Role model
- Trailblazer
- Innovative
- Visionary
- Diplomatic
- Assertive
- Creative in business
- Public speaker
- Lecturer
- Risk-taker
- Negotiator
- Mediator
- Persuader
- Talker
- Outgoing
- Social
- Motivator
- Manifestor
- Rule enforcer
- Lawmaker
- Team player
- Troubleshooter
- Healer, medical
- Healer, natural
- Psychic
- Medium
- Entertainer
- Hard-working
- Emotionally strong
- Physically strong
- Energetic
- Brave
- Adventurous
- Dedicated
- Follows through
- Reliable
- Disciplined
- Detail-orientated
- Organized
- Focused
- Mathematical
- Analytical
- Intellectual
- Empathic
- Sensitive
- Compassionate
- Good listener
- Easygoing
- Patient
- Caring
- Cautious
- Friendly
- Comical
- Fun
- Optimistic
- Fixer
- Positive
- Forgiving
- Generous
- Honest
- Loyal
- Dependable
- Down-to-earth
- Inventive
- Resourceful
- Spiritually connected
- Balanced
- Open-minded
- Inspiring
- Motivational
- Fair
- Honest
- Planner
- Persistent
- Teacher
- Professor
- Academic
- Disciplinarian
- Messenger
- Comforting
- Supportive
- Caregiver
- Good with animals
- Promoter
- Good with children
- Understanding

Use the space below to add additional Life Tools that are not listed. Also add any words that better describe a Life Tool you have:

EXERCISES TO HELP IDENTIFY YOUR LIFE TOOLS

Find Tools in Your Achievements

Think about the moments in your life when you achieved something that you are proud of. It can be something for which you received great recognition, such as winning a race or being honored for an accomplishment. It can also be more personal, such as feeling like you got through a difficult time, made great leaps in your learning, or reconciled a relationship. Now think about the Life Tools or traits that helped you to achieve these. Perhaps there is a Life Tool that you developed through this experience. Write down the achievement and the Life Tool that you used or developed.

_____

_____

_____

_____

_____

_____

_____

You will probably find that you already have these marked on your Life Tools list. If you've found any new ones, add them now to your Life Tools list.

Find Life Tools in the People You Admire

Make a list of people you admire and what specific personality traits or attributes they have that you admire. They can be famous or those whom you know personally, such as an old school teacher, a friend, a relative, or an acquaintance. It can even be someone you only met once. Who you choose does not matter. It is the trait that you admire that is important.

Do not choose someone for what they have or where they are in their life, meaning don't admire someone because they have a big house or a fancy sports car. Though you can admire the personality trait or Life Tool that enabled them to achieve this abundance and/or maintain it. For example, admiring someone because they inherited a million dollars doesn't count. Admiring someone for having made a million dollars because you admire their hard work or tenacity means you admire those Life Tools. Make a list of the people you admire. Then, next to each person's name, write the trait or Life Tool that you admire.

....
NOTE: Finish this exercise completely before reading the next section.
....

Now reread the list you just made about those whom you admire, looking only at the traits or Life Tools. These are Life Tools that you possess! Yes! You can only recognize the Life Tools in someone else that you possess yourself or you wouldn't be able to recognize it. You may think that everyone must admire that person for that trait, but you would be very surprised to find out otherwise.

When I do workshops, people choose a variety of celebrities and well-known individuals (as well as those in their own family), but what they admire in the person is very different. Two of my clients might admire the same celebrity, but the trait that each client holds in high esteem is completely different. People choose specific traits because they, themselves, have them. We are a reflection of one another and you can only admire a trait in someone else if you have it yourself. You wouldn't even know what it was if you did not posses it as well. I know this sounds unbelievable, but it is true. If you don't think you have that Life Tool, then perhaps you have not yet developed it, but you do have it within yourself; you have the potential for that Life Tool.

Sometimes the answers will surprise you. A man in one of my workshops shared that he admired Mother Teresa. When I asked him why, he said it was because (1) she dealt with the poorest communities, and (2) she dealt with people that no one else wanted to deal with and throughout it all, she had compassion. When I told him these were his traits, he looked puzzled. So I inquired what he did for a living. He replied he was a police officer. Did I need to point out that he (1) deals with the poorest communities and (2) deals with people no one else wants to deal with! We called him Office Mother Teresa for the remainder of the workshop!

Now go back to your Life Tools list and add or emphasize the ones you have now discovered; the ones you recognized in someone else because they are yours!

Find Tools in What Others See in You

What do your friends say that you are good at? What attributes or Life Tools have your friends commented that you have? Often other people see us better than we can see ourselves. They can more easily observe us because they aren't clouded by the negative inner dialogue we have a tendency to ruminate on; thus they may see our Life Tools more clearly.

My own life offers a great example of a Life Tool that others recognized in me first. Never in a million years would I have thought that I could write. I wasn't very good in English class and I can't even spell! When I started to write, it was out of a desire to share my spiritual insights; I thought the writing itself would be terrible. My friends told me how much they loved my down-to-earth writing style that made them feel like they were really there. My mom reminded me that when I was young, I used to write letters and they were always so natural and fun. It was through their awareness of this trait as well as their encouragement that I decided to write and publish. I never would have thought on my own to do it.

As you make your own list of tools that others see in you, a word of caution: Make sure that you don't include Life Tools another wishes you to possess. If it is your father's desire that you follow in his footsteps and take over the family business or continue in the same profession, he may be projecting a Life Tool upon you. Make sure that what you add to your list is something another sees in you and they haven't been clouded by personal motives. Sometimes a parent genuinely sees a Life Tool in you, but at other times, they are projecting their own desires.

Your family, friends, and co-workers will often have honest, complimentary observations about your Life Tools. Leave your modesty behind and write down what others say you are good at.

_____
_____
_____
_____
_____

Go ahead and add these to your Life Tools list, even if you are not completely in agreement.

Find Tools in Your Physical Attributes

What physical attributes do you have? Are you tall? Short? Do you have long fingers? A low center of gravity? Your attributes, even ones that you may think of as negative, are all part of your toolbox. The benefits of some may be obvious, while others you may not initially realize are strengths.

What attributes do you recognize? What do others say about you? Are you extremely limber or double-jointed? Can you put your feet behind your head? It may seem like a party trick to you, but perhaps you can parlay this gift into work as an acrobat, dancer, or performer. Your audience can emotionally connect and share in the joy and appreciation of how expressive and incredible a gift the physical body is.

Make sure not to filter your list or be too modest. For example, if you were born good-looking, this is a Life Tool. If you are meant to be a news anchor, odds are that you'll have an easier time breaking in if you are attractive. It is not bad to acknowledge that you're attractive or that you know how to appeal to the opposite sex as there is probably a purpose in it. Princess Diana was known for her commitment to her charity work and used her beauty, as well as her royal standing, to increase public awareness of her causes. Angelina Jolie has the same blessing of beauty to use.

If life has given you quirky or interesting looks, that could be a Life Tool as well. Some of our most successful actors and actresses have very distinctive and unique looks that differentiate them and capture the imagination of audiences. Similarly, character actors parlay their distinctive looks into memorable roles.

Your physical size and characteristics are all Tools. If your Purpose is to touch people through the game of basketball, you've likely been given the Life Tool of great height. (Although there are some "short" basketball players who are given the Purpose of showing others that with hard work and passion, you can beat the odds and live your dream.) A pianist may be blessed with the Life Tool of long, slender fingers. Were you born physically strong? Agile? Ambidextrous? Fast?

Now list the Life Tools you were born with. If you aren't sure of your Tools, include ones that others have told you that you have. Remember, to get the most out of this book, don't filter out any Life Tools because you are trying to be humble; they are all part of your Toolbox.

_____

_____

_____

_____

Now add these to your Life Tools List.

Find Tools in What Irks You about Others

What do people do that really irritates you? Do you say, "I can't stand people who are lacking in common sense," or "I dislike people who are flaky or disorganized"? Perhaps you think, "I don't like it when people don't keep their word." Think about what traits annoy you in other people.

You don't like these things because they are the opposite of a Life Tool that you have. If not, you simply wouldn't care. What they are doing goes against your Life Tools and your path and your subconscious lets you know. List what irks you that others do and think about what the opposite of this trait could be. For example, if you don't like it when people do something in a rush or try to rush you, perhaps one of your Life Tools is to be a planner, to think deliberately and carefully, being attentive to every detail. Perhaps you get irritated when people tell little "white lies." Your Life Tool could be integrity and honor.

Write down what annoys you and what could be its opposite, which is your Life Tool.

_____

_____

_____

_____

Now add these to your Life Tools List.

Find Tools in Your Faults

Make a list of what you perceive your faults to be. What holds you back? Do you have a fault that keeps you from accomplishing your goals? Is there an aspect of your personality that stops you from doing the things you'd like to do? Write each fault as a negative trait. Some examples are: worrier, impatient, obsessive, hot-tempered, pessimistic, insecure, having a negative inner dialogue. To find your faults you can also look at what you would like to do or actions you would like to take, but your faults are holding you back. Ask yourself, "I would like to _____ but I am too _____ [timid, cynical, risk-averse, etc.]"

List your faults below before continuing with the chapter.

_____

_____

_____

_____

_____

Now that you've listed your faults, look for their positive side. What I mean by this is to ask yourself: What good could come out of each fault? What Life Tools could you be hiding? Shyness may help you to be empathic, understanding, approachable, or reflective. Obsessive may help you to be detail-oriented, organized, analytical, or focused.

Sometimes it's helpful to look at the opposite meaning of the fault. For example, if you are pessimistic about your skills, why are you? Are there positive traits relating to why you are a pessimist? For instance, if you think that your work won't be good enough, the positive could be being a perfectionist. If you are pessimistic because you don't think you'll be able to compete the task, the opposite could be having excellent follow-through. If your concern is that you don't have the depth of understanding, you could be masking a talent for research. Also think about what others have told you that they perceive as your faults. Again, see what hidden positive Life Tools you can find.

Write down the positive Life Tools you've found hidden in your faults. Remember, you may just now be identifying them, so even if they are potential Life Tools that you have not yet developed, they are still to be included below.

_____

_____

_____

_____

Now add these to your Life Tools List.

Find Tools in Your Fears

Do your fears keep you from accomplishing your goals? Is there something that you are afraid of but would love to do? It may be a Life Tool that you haven't perfected yet. I used to be absolutely terrified of public speaking and admired those who could do it. The few times I had been asked to speak, I would sit in the bathroom beforehand feeling like I was going to throw up. When I started teaching mediumship, I found that public speaking wasn't so bad. In fact, pretty soon I even started to like it. I felt at home in front a group and even as the crowds became larger, it was no longer scary. My passion for public speaking grew. Now I absolutely love it!

Write down the positive Life Tools that you would like to cultivate but are currently too afraid to.

_____

_____

_____

_____

Now add these to your Life Tools List.

As in the previous section, you are also going to look to the opposite of your fears to see if there is a positive Life Tool hidden behind it. For example, are you afraid of standing up for yourself? Maybe you actually have a hidden talent for advocacy and standing up for those members of society who have no voice.

Make a list of what you perceive your "fears" to be. It may be helpful to fill in the following sentence to help you identify your fears. "I would like to _____ but I am too afraid of _____ [talking to people I don't know, being wrong, looking stupid, failing, etc.]."

_____
_____
_____
_____
_____

Write down the positive Life Tools that are hidden in your fears.

_____
_____
_____
_____

Now add these to your Life Tools List.

Find Tools in Your Relationships

What are the important relationships in your life? Are you a sister, mother, wife, daughter, cousin, mother-in-law, or aunt? Are you a father, brother, son, husband, uncle, or father-in-law? How do you feel about each role? Is there a relationship that you feel particularly strongly about? Is this in a positive or negative way? What positive traits or Life Tools are exhibited in these relationships? For instance, if you are a mother, does it bring out your Life Tools of being caring, nurturing, empathizing, and teaching? Does it also reveal impatience or feeling overwhelmed? As we did in the previous section, what positives can you find in the negative aspects? Perhaps impatience is teaching you how to be patient or more tolerant. Perhaps it reveals an ability for multitasking or organizing.

Is there a particularly bad relationship that you feel strongly about? Could it reveal a Life Tool? For instance, if you feel that your mother treats you horribly, how has this helped you develop positive Life Tools? Does it make you a more caring mother to your own children? Does it make you more independent or driven?

Write down the relationship and any positive Life Tools you find.

_____
_____
_____
_____
_____
_____
_____

Now add these to your Life Tools List.

Your Final Life Tools List

At this point you may have a large list of Life Tools, some of which really stand out in importance and others that seem to be lesser Tools. You may also have more than one word describing the same Life Tool. If this is the case, try to choose the best word that fits this Life Tool.

The next step is to decide which are your major Life Tools. Try to choose the 3-5 Life Tools that resonate the most. You may find it helpful to ask of each one, "Could I live without this specific Life Tool?" They may the ones that you are currently using most often. Alternatively, are there Life Tools that you feel you aren't using as much as you should be? As you're doing this workbook, which ones seem to stand out more and more? Perhaps there are Tools that resonated more before you started this workbook, and now you aren't sure. After having done these exercises and contemplated your answers, which Life Tools now stand out as the most important?

The other Life Tools on your list are not being discarded. They may be potential Life Tools that you'll use in the future, ones that you are using for your lesser theme, or ones that are just being used for a short period (e.g., to resolves a specific karmic situation).

List your top 3-5 Life Tools below.

_____
_____
_____
_____
_____

• •

These Life Tools are what you are using when you are living your True Purpose. Now we are going to try to discover how to use these Tools so that you can more clearly understand your True Purpose.

• •

THEMES

Finding Your Themes

As you reflect on your life, you will start to see Themes; that is you will seem drawn to people and circumstances that seem to be a recurrence. You will find that even in differing areas of your life, you appear to be playing the same role or are having similar experiences. Themes are a part of our mission in life, our True Purpose. Our True Purpose can be made up of more than one Theme. For instance, we may have one Theme that is the strongest and then have additional lesser Themes.

Often there are recurring Themes that play out over and over in different ways in our lives. As we recognize the Themes that repeat, we can discover our overall True Purpose. Your Themes will usually represent what you are good at and will include your Life Tools. As you identify your Themes, you'll likely find that they are related to the Life Tools you've already found.

Your Themes List

Your Themes will be individual to you. However, the following list of examples may help you to better understand what you are looking for. You want to identify the Themes in your life that are important or keep recurring. The ones you will be listing here should be positive. We will get to any negative ones in a moment.

If you think any of the Themes listed below apply to you, go ahead and mark them. If others come to mind that are not on this list, write them in the space below. You are going to be using this list quite a bit, so you may prefer to make copies to use as a worksheet.

Sample Themes

- People come to me for advice on relationship/family/career issues.
- Caring for and protecting animals.
- Being a mentor.

- Keeping everyone organized.
- Caring for and helping children.
- Speaking up for those who are unable to do so themselves.
- Inspiring people.
- Finding creative solutions.
- Never giving up, no matter how difficult the obstacle.
- Diffusing tense situations and helping people come to an amicable solution.
- Being a leader, especially when challenges arise.
- Being the one people can rely on.
- I have a calming effect on people.
- I am good at managing people.
- I like to organize groups.
- I'm good at rallying others together in support of a cause/charity/issue.
- I fix broken objects and things.
- Using my creative talents as a healing tool.
- Connecting with and compassionately supporting those in need.
- Finding beauty in things and displaying it to the world.
- Being a good listener, which helps the person to heal.
- Finding humor in situations and making people laugh.
- Raising people's awareness of social issues.
- Helping those in need.
- Making people smile and bringing joy to those around me.
- Lightening the mood and soothing upset feelings.
- I enjoy assisting the elderly.

Add your Themes below:

EXERCISES TO HELP IDENTIFY YOUR THEMES

Find Themes in a Negative Condition

Some of the themes that jump out at you or immediately come to mind might actually be negative conditions. These often contradict our Theme and are actually there to test us or are lessons we are going through in order to perfect our Theme.

Sample Negative Conditions

- I let others control me.
- I am always left out or left until last.
- I had to endure a difficult health issue.
- I had to endure abuse in my childhood.
- I have to do things myself or they aren't done right.
- I feel that I am not loved.
- I have a difficult time controlling my anger.
- I take on too many things.
- I take on other people's worries or issues.
- I have issues with my weight or have an addiction.
- I seem to have constant financial problems.
- I am continually hurt in relationships.
- I feel unappreciated.

It takes a little more effort, but if you dig deep, you can probably find something positive that comes out of your negative conditions. For instance, a negative condition could be "I let others control me." A positive trait or Theme could be "I am a good team player." Alternatively, it could be that you no longer allow a specific negative condition to affect you and this growth leads to a positive, opposite theme. For example, "I help people who are in abusive situations because I have been through it myself and I understand the dynamic." A negative condition of "I feel I am not loved" could be a reflection that you are searching for love and the positive Theme could be "to learn to appreciate and love myself."

List any negative conditions that you feel you have in your life.

_____

_____

_____

_____

_____

Are these something that you are working on? In what way could they indicate a positive theme?

_____

_____

_____

_____

_____

Add the positive Themes you found to your Themes List.

Find Themes in Your Major Life Moments

Think about the moments in your life when you felt great, when you felt truly happy and connected. It could be a moment where something significant happened, or it could be simply when you were meditating in the garden or watching your children play. Were you using any Life Tools at these particular moments? What Themes can you derive from these moments?

For example, you felt truly connected when you were leading a group of young people. They came to you for advice and you used your Life Tools of understanding, empathy, and helping people to feel at ease. You recognize that one of your Themes is people come to you when they are distressed and you help them to feel calm and at ease.

Perhaps you were honored for your achievements in raising money for a charity. In this case you used your Life Tools of being a good communicator and humanitarian to enable you to raise the money. This Theme could be to stand up for the rights of those in need.

Even seemingly mundane examples can be important. It might be that you helped a neighbor clean up and organize their garage. You used your organizational skills and your love of hard work. When it was finished, you felt like you had really accomplished something and their gratitude was so rewarding. Perhaps one of your Themes is you attract organizational projects that makes other's lives easier.

You may have an epiphany about your Theme while watching your daughter in a school play. You know how hard she worked to overcome her fear and realize how you, as a parent, were supportive and instrumental to her success. You recognize that one of your Themes may be to encourage, motivate, and support others, be it as a parent or with other people in your life.

Write the moment and what you can derive as a Theme.

_____
_____
_____
_____
_____

Add the positive Themes you found to your Themes List.

Find Themes in Positive Life Events

Review the timeline of your life from birth to the present and consider each significant positive life event. Reflect on every major achievement and the important moments—ones you consider to be positive (we'll get to the negative ones later). Don't skip your early childhood as this is the period when you were actually closer to your True Purpose. As you note each life event, ask yourself, "Could this have been a time when I was living my True Purpose? Did I feel in sync with life, as if I had some kind of higher purpose? Or did an event change the direction of my life? Was I using my Life Tools?"

Reflect on your childhood. Did you have positive experiences at school? Did you enjoy a hobby? Was there another area of your early life that was particularly positive? Did positive relationships come into your life? Did you move or travel to a place that was a positive experience?

Think about the positive experiences you had growing up, starting school, learning to drive, moving away from home, getting your first place to live, etc. Consider your jobs and other roles in life. Could any of these positive major life events have shaped your True Purpose? If so, in what way? What Themes do they have?

_____

_____

_____

_____

_____

_____

Add the positive Themes you found to your Themes List.

Find Themes in Negative Life Events

Think about the timeline of your life from birth to the present and review each significant, difficult, or negative life event. Especially consider the ones from early childhood. Even if there is an event which you are not quite sure actually happened, be sure to include it. Sometimes our early memories are fuzzy, or we don't specifically recall an event, but just have a "feeling" that it happened. Events from our formative years can be very significant.

As you grew up, what major difficult events affected you? Family problems? Difficult relationships? The loss of a loved one? Financial Issues? Be sure to also consider events that may seem insignificant to others but you still carry negative thoughts about it. Perhaps you felt a lack of love or attention when someone didn't say or do something. It could be something as simple as a parent being in a rush and forgetting to say goodbye when they left for work. It may have seemed insignificant to them, but if you still feel a twinge of emotional distress about it years later, it is important to include.

Write the event and the "feeling" you had with the experience.

_____
_____
_____
_____
_____
_____
_____
_____

Now that you've identified the negative events from your life and the feelings that each one evoked, what did you discover? Is there a positive Theme you can find in each event? Can you determine how these events may have strengthened your main Theme? For instance, did you learn something? Did it lead you to do the opposite, which was more positive or constructive? Did it make you more determined?

The following examples show how a negative event can become part of a Theme. For instance, if your father got fired, leaving your family in financial straits, did you learn how to support yourself through any circumstance? Did you develop the drive to never give up? Another example might be if a parent left or died and you ended up taking care of younger siblings, perhaps you developed a love of caring for children. Your Theme might be to help guide and care for children who lack established support systems or families.

As you reflect on each difficult period, you'll also want to ask yourself if the event appears to be related to your True Purpose or if it is karmic in nature. Or does the difficulty appear to be a random blockage? Could it simply be an opportunity to serve others? Does it appear to be resolving karma that may or may not be related to your True Purpose?

What have you discovered about the difficult events in your life? If you are not sure of an event's meaning, sit quietly and ask for guidance. You may not be able to get an immediate answer for everything. It is ok to reflect on it again later to see what new intuitions come. Also note whether you think each difficult period was related to your Theme or if it was a separate karmic event.

_____

_____

_____

_____

_____

Add the positive Themes you've found to your Themes List.

Themes in Your Relationships

See if you can recognize Themes in your relationships. For example, you may notice that you are often the moderator in family disagreements and tend to be the balanced one who is able to keep the peace and bring both sides to an agreement. Perhaps you are the nurturing, caring one whom others come to when in need. This Theme may be to help those in distress. Maybe you are the comedic one in your family, helping to bring joy to people's lives through laughter.

Do any of your relationships contribute to or reflect Themes?

_____
_____
_____
_____
_____
_____

If you feel that some of these relationships are not part of your Theme, but rather isolated incidents of karma playing out, write them below. Note that these are differentiated as karmic lessons.

_____
_____
_____
_____
_____

Add the positive Themes you've found to your Themes List.

Themes in What Irks You about Others

Think about what other people do or say that really annoys you. Do people who act ignorant or lazy bother you? If one of your Themes is to teach and motivate people, you can bet that these people will annoy you. They irk you because they are going against your Theme. Think about what irks you and then look for the opposite, which might indicate a Theme for you.

_____

_____

_____

_____

Add the positive Themes you've found to your Themes List.

Themes in When People Ask You for Help

Are people always asking you for help? Do people share their problems with you or feel like they can confide in you even when it is unprompted? Perhaps one of your Themes is to heal people through the spoken word. Or it could be that you are meant to be a hands-on healer working through compassion. Perhaps one of your Themes is to fix mechanical things to help make people's lives easier.

When do you feel most appreciated by others? Other people often unconsciously know what your True Purpose is and may recruit you to help them. You are also subconsciously attracting people whom you may serve through your True Purpose. Ask yourself: What am I doing for others? When do I feel most loved and appreciated?

_____

_____

_____

_____

_____

Does any of what you've listed reflect a Theme or give you more clarity as to what your True Purpose is?

_____

_____

_____

_____

Add the positive Themes you've found to your Themes List.

Find Themes in Your Past Projects

Reflect on your favorite jobs, projects, and endeavors. Think about jobs you've had or specific aspects of a job that particularly resonated. It could be a project that you worked on, something you made happen, help you provided to a person, or another endeavor. Perhaps a project from your youth, a summer job, or a school project made an impact. For example, perhaps your high school had a mentoring program and you discovered that you have a talent for connecting with children from challenging backgrounds. Maybe your job included customer service and you found out that you have a knack for diplomatically solving problems and soothing upset feelings.

Why did you love your favorite jobs and projects? Did you feel Divinely connected while you were doing them? Were you using your Life Tools? As you reflect, what Themes come to mind?

Write your favorite jobs and projects and the Themes they may reflect.

_____

_____

_____

_____

_____

_____

Add the positive Themes you've found to your Themes List.

Find Themes in Your Perfect Job

If you could do any job, what would it be? Make sure it's not a job or career that a parent or someone else wants you to do. It should be something that you really desire. For our purpose, assume that money or training is not an issue. What job would you be willing to do for free? It doesn't have to be a "normal" job. It could even be a made up position.

Use your imagination. Does your dream job involve exploration and adventure? Do you want to travel the world as a photographer or humanitarian? Do you want to help heal others? Perhaps you want to work with dolphins and whales. Maybe your perfect job involves making a difference in the lives of children. Or do you want to be a surfer who writes poetry? It could be anything you desire.

Visualize your perfect job. What Themes can you identify? Note the job and its related Themes below.

_____

_____

_____

_____

Add the positive Themes you've found to your Themes List.

Find Themes in Your Interests

What are your interests? What activities do you enjoy doing? This isn't just about hobbies. What subjects do you like to talk about the most? What kinds of books do you enjoy reading? What were your interests when you were younger? Where would you like to live? What kind of lifestyle would make you really happy? What Themes show up in these interests?

For example, if you enjoy hiking and being in nature, perhaps your Theme is to bring more awareness to how we treat the environment. If you enjoy reading, perhaps your Theme is to inspire people to use their imagination and dream.

_____

_____

_____

_____

_____

_____

_____

_____

Add the positive themes you've found to your Themes List.

Your Final Themes List

Now go back and review your Themes List, which includes the Themes that you've identified through the workbook exercises. Find the phrases that encompass the main Themes you have found. You may have a main Theme and one or two secondary Themes. You may also find that some Themes appear to be in conflict, but actually they are a test or an obstacle to the same Theme. Perhaps all your Themes are really the same thing. Maybe you feel that you have two or more main Themes.

You want to try to formulate a sentence or two that encompasses your main

Theme. If you feel strongly about any secondary Themes, you may include these as well. Once you come up with your sentence/s, sit quietly and meditate. Feel how your sentence resonates. You can "try it on" so to speak to see if the sentence/s really fit.

_____
_____
_____
_____
_____
_____

Your True Purpose Statement

Now you will be crafting a statement that describes your True Purpose. You are going to incorporate both the main Themes and the Life Tools that you found. You want your True Purpose Statement to be essentially one sentence in length, though it can be a long sentence or perhaps a two-part sentence (at the most).

As you dig deep, search to put words to your True Purpose. You want to define the meaning of your True Purpose and put it into a sentence or statement about your life path. It is okay if you end up changing the final wording; it is the process of discovering yourself that's important. This sentence will help you to better understand the meaning of your True Purpose or mission. The words will serve to remind you of this Purpose.

As you formulate your sentence, remember that your True Purpose is also going to be a means through which you will serve. This service to others may be friends and family, children, or the masses. Perhaps it will be to help animals, the environment, or Mother Earth. Our True Purpose brings us great pleasure and satisfaction, but it also serves others. Make sure that when you formulate your statement, it expresses a way in which you serve.

As well as serving others, you are also serving and nurturing a need in yourself. Your True Purpose is going to be something that you enjoy and love doing.

Remember, your Purpose is never going to be "to experience being miserable" or "to be poor" or "be unwanted." It'll be nothing of the kind, so don't give in to self-pity. Your Purpose could be to get through a challenge and achieve something, but it is never just to be in pain or poverty. Remember, it is for the highest good for yourself and others.

What you've learned from doing the exercises in the previous chapters will help you to craft your statement. Remember, you can change it later if you discover that it needs tweaking, but for now, make your best effort to encapsulate your True Purpose thus far. It is not so much the actual words that are important, but the process that is bringing clarity for you to feel and resonate with your True Purpose.

Play around with statements that include your Themes and your Life Tools. Then "try them on." Ask yourself how you feel about that Purpose. If it is your True Purpose, it will "feel" right. The next section includes examples of True Purpose Statements, but please do not look ahead as it is more helpful to create your own first. Afterward, you may look at the subsequent examples.

_____

_____

_____

_____

_____

_____

_____

_____

_____

_____

TRUE PURPOSE STATEMENT EXAMPLES

The following are examples of True Purpose Statements. However, each of us is a complex human being with a very individual True Purpose, so each of us will have our own unique statement. I've provided these to help you as you to continue fine-tune your statement. Some of these examples may resonate with you (either the whole sentence or just part of it). If you find a sentence or a part of a sentence that you think fits, meditate on it. Sit quietly with the words and repeat them in your mind. Do they resonate with your soul? Mark any that resonate.

My True Purpose is

- To express beauty through art, photography, and other creative mediums.
- To help people appreciate the arts and connect with their own creativity through my work as an artist/teacher/writer/…
- To be a loving, caring parent while finding balance in my career.
- To help others feel less stressed and anxious by pointing out the humor in life.
- To help people to heal by teaching them how to actively participate in their own healing.
- To teach people how to live more harmonious, balanced lives.
- To be an advocate for animal rights, using my skills of public speaking, advocacy, and the ability to emotionally move people.
- To be an advocate for human rights, using my determination, drive to succeed despite the odds, and compassion.
- To help people become more organized and efficient to make their day-to-day lives easier.
- To use the written word to humorously help people with their relationships.

- To encourage learning and the creative expression of youths, while keeping them within a structured framework.
- To research and organize information for the dissemination of knowledge to the world.
- To use my understanding of how things work to fix mechanical things, which makes people's lives easier.
- To be an inventor so I can help to improve the quality of people's lives.
- To help people to discover their innate healing abilities and thus help to spread healing to the world.
- To provide comfort to those who are dying through care, humor, and spiritual support.
- To connect people with their passion for life through music.
- To design/construct houses and buildings that are practical, environmentally conscious, and esthetically pleasing.
- To find innovative, harmonious, and creative solutions to societal issues.
- To help the disabled to receive proper care and greater respect.
- To help people resolve family issues through helping them to see the other person's perspective and be able to come to a place of understanding and forgiveness.
- Motivating people to take care of their physical bodies through my own example of physical ability and athletic prowess.
- To heal others through talking, listening, and compassionate discourse.
- Through my own example, to show that the most difficult challenges in life can be overcome.
- To be a connector of people in the business world and to help them to form symbiotic networks.
- To expand people's awareness of their own possibilities through exposing them to what others have been able to accomplish, create, and overcome.

- To protect and preserve historical artifacts to enhance our cultural awareness.
- Through my example and sharing my experiences, I can help people to become more compassionate and loving.
- To be a negotiator and help people to reach harmonious, fair, and satisfying resolutions.
- To help people to be more understanding and compassionate of religious and cultural differences.
- Through my own example and experiences, to help people to overcome their addictions.
- To help people to develop self-love by teaching them how to love and cherish themselves.
- To take care of Mother Earth and the environment.
- To help people to realize their true potential through spiritual awareness.
- To help educate people in how to heal their physical bodies through good nutrition.
- To comfort and help people to heal their grief and trauma.
- To educate through public speaking.
- To guide people in their life choices.

Consider the sentence that you formulated in the previous section as well as the examples above as you continue to fine-tune your True Purpose Statement.

_____

_____

_____

_____

TEST THE TRUTH OF YOUR TRUE PURPOSE STATEMENT

Your body can be used as a pendulum to test if something is true or resonates as positive for you. Essentially what you are doing is using your subconscious to show a reaction in your body. This is very easy to do. Stand in a relaxed position with your feet about shoulder-width apart. Quiet your mind and center yourself. Ask yourself a yes or no question, such as, "Is it true that [insert question]?" If the statement is true or the answer is yes, then your body will tilt forward. If the statement is not true or the answer is no, your body will lean away or backward.

Now you will test your True Purpose Statement. Stand in a relaxed position and say your True Purpose Statement (aloud or silently). If the statement resonates well with your subconscious, your body will lean forward. If your body sways backward, then there is something in the statement that you either have a hard time believing or it just doesn't sit right with you. For example, you could say, "Is it true that my True Purpose is to motivate people to take care of their physical body through healthy nutrition?" If this is your True Purpose or a part of your Purpose, that is this statement feels good and true to your Higher Self, then your body should lean forward. If your body leans backward, then experiment with the wording of your statement to see if you can get a more positive response from your Higher Self.

DOES YOUR TRUE PURPOSE MATCH YOUR MAP?

As previously discussed, when you are born, you are born into a family, geographic location, and circumstances that fit the environment you'll need to carry out your True Purpose. Your genealogy and ancestry will fit your Purpose, not the other way around. Your astrology will fit perfectly with the personality and tools that you will need. Likewise, the numerology of both your date of birth and your name will have the vibration that you'll need. We'll now check if you are in sync with your astrology, numerology, and other aspects of the "map" you were born with.

ASTROLOGY AND YOUR TRUE PURPOSE

The North Node

After choosing your True Purpose in Heaven, you are born into a life with an astrology chart to match what you plan to accomplish. Your personality traits and the gifts you are born with will be mapped out in your chart and reflected in your Life Tools.

There are points in an astrology chart called Nodes–the North Node and the South Node. These are mathematical points where the moon's orbit crosses the ecliptic (the path of the sun through the sky). In your natal chart (your birth chart), the North Node is thought to show your True Purpose. Many astrologers believe it represents our destiny or karma. In my workshops I've found that many of my students find that their North Node directly relates to their True Purpose Statement. The North Node often represents what we should be learning or completing in this lifetime. However, many times people don't start working on this until later in life. Again, this is because often they are not so aware of their Purpose until mid-life.

Your South Node exactly opposes your North Node, so the astrological sign of your South Node is always the opposite sign from your North Node. The South Node represents your Tools or an old Purpose from a past life that you've already accomplished. It may be something you fall back on because it feels comfortable or it seems easy and familiar to you. It can sometime be a crutch because your North Node traits feel like something new and perhaps harder to learn whereas your South Node traits are things you know you are good at.

Of course, there are also other areas of your natal chart that represent your personality, Life Tools, and life path. You chose your natal chart before birth to include your major and minor themes and your unresolved karma. You also chose to be born at a certain date and time in order for your natal chart to reflect your True Purpose. Even if your parents influenced the time of your birth (e.g., a scheduled cesarean section), this, too, was predetermined by you and your guides.

The following table can be used to look up the astrological sign of your North and South Node.

North and South Node Table

DATE		NORTH NODE	SOUTH NODE
February 8, 1921-	August 22, 1922	Libra	Aries
August 23, 1922-	August 27, 1922	Virgo	Pisces
August 28, 1922-	August 31, 1922	Libra	Aries
September 1, 1922-	April 22, 1924	Virgo	Pisces
April 23, 1924-	October 26, 1925	Leo	Aquarius
October 27, 1925-	April 16, 1927	Cancer	Capricorn
April 17, 1927-	December 28, 1928	Gemini	Sagittarius
December 29, 1928-	July 7, 1930	Taurus	Scorpio
July 8, 1930-	December 28, 1931	Aries	Libra
December 29, 1931-	July 24, 1933	Pisces	Virgo
July 25, 1933-	March 8, 1935	Aquarius	Leo
March 9, 1935-	September 14, 1936	Capricorn	Cancer
September 15, 1936-	March 3, 1938	Sagittarius	Gemini
March 4, 1938-	September 11, 1939	Scorpio	Taurus
September 12, 1939-	May 24, 1941	Libra	Aries
May 25, 1941-	November 21, 1942	Virgo	Pisces
November 22, 1942-	May 11, 1944	Leo	Aquarius
May 12, 1944-	December 2, 1945	Cancer	Capricorn
December 3, 1945-	August 2, 1947	Gemini	Sagittarius
August 3, 1947-	January 25, 1949	Taurus	Scorpio
January 26, 1949-	July 26, 1950	Aries	Libra
July 27, 1950-	March 28, 1952	Pisces	Virgo
March 29, 1952-	October 9, 1953	Aquarius	Leo
October 10, 1953-	April 2, 1955	Capricorn	Cancer
April 3, 1955-	October 4, 1956	Sagittarius	Gemini
October 5, 1956-	June 16, 1958	Scorpio	Taurus
June 17, 1958-	December 15, 1959	Libra	Aries
December 16, 1959-	June 10, 1961	Virgo	Pisces
June 11, 1961-	December 23, 1962	Leo	Aquarius

December 24, 1962-	August 25, 1964	Cancer	Capricorn
August 26, 1964-	February 19, 1966	Gemini	Sagittarius
February 20, 1966-	August 19, 1967	Taurus	Scorpio
August 20, 1967-	April 19, 1969	Aries	Libra
April 20, 1969-	November 2, 1970	Pisces	Virgo
November 3, 1970-	April 27, 1972	Aquarius	Leo
April 28, 1972-	October 26, 1973	Capricorn	Cancer
October 27, 1973-	July 9, 1975	Sagittarius	Gemini
July 10, 1975-	January 7, 1977	Scorpio	Taurus
January 8, 1977-	July 5, 1978	Libra	Aries
July 6, 1978-	January 5, 1980	Virgo	Pisces
January 6, 1980-	January 6, 1980	Leo	Aquarius
January 7, 1980-	January 12, 1980	Virgo	Pisces
January 13, 1980-	September 24, 1981	Leo	Aquarius
September 25, 1981-	March 15, 1983	Cancer	Capricorn
March 16, 1983-	September 11, 1984	Gemini	Sagittarius
September 12, 1984-	April 6, 1986	Taurus	Scorpio
April 7, 1986-	May 5, 1986	Aries	Libra
May 6, 1986-	May 8, 1986	Taurus	Scorpio
May 9, 1986-	December 2, 1987	Aries	Libra
December 3, 1987-	May 22, 1989	Pisces	Virgo
May 23, 1989-	November 18, 1990	Aquarius	Leo
November 19, 1990-	August 1, 1992	Capricorn	Cancer
August 2, 1992-	February 1, 1994	Sagittarius	Gemini
February 2, 1994-	July 31, 1995	Scorpio	Taurus
August 1, 1995-	January 24, 1997	Libra	Aries
January 25, 1997-	October 20, 1998	Virgo	Pisces
October 21, 1998-	April 8, 2000	Leo	Aquarius
April 9, 2000-	October 12, 2001	Cancer	Capricorn
October 13, 2001-	April 13, 2003	Gemini	Sagittarius
April 14, 2003-	December 26, 2004	Taurus	Scorpio
December 27, 2004-	June 22, 2006	Aries	Libra

Part 2: Finding Your True Purpose

June 23, 2006-	December 14, 2007	Pisces	Virgo
December 15, 2007-	August 21, 2009	Aquarius	Leo
August 22, 2009-	March 3, 2011	Capricorn	Cancer
March 4, 2011-	August 29, 2012	Sagittarius	Gemini
August 29, 2012-	February 18, 2014	Scorpio	Taurus
February 19, 2014-	November 11, 2015	Libra	Aries
November 12, 2015-	May 9, 2017	Virgo	Pisces
May 10, 2017-	November 6, 2018	Leo	Aquarius
November 7, 2018-	May 5, 2020	Cancer	Capricorn
May 6, 2020-	January 18, 2022	Gemini	Sagittarius
January 19, 2022-	July 17, 2023	Taurus	Scorpio
July 18, 2023-	January 11, 2025	Aries	Libra
January 12, 2025-	July 26, 2026	Pisces	Virgo
July 27, 2026-	March 26, 2028	Aquarius	Leo
March 27, 2028-	September 23, 2029	Capricorn	Cancer

HOW THE SIGN OF YOUR NORTH AND SOUTH NODE AFFECTS YOU

The astrological sign of your North Node is an indicator of your True Purpose. The astrological sign of your South Node represents a previous Purpose that you've learned already and now comes easily to you. Perhaps it even distracts you because it is more comfortable or familiar than your North Node. For example, if your North Node is in Cancer and your Purpose in this life relates to being a parent and your home life, but your previous Purpose (South Node in Capricorn) was being in business and a leader, you may find learning to be a parent is your theme. Perhaps parenting is more challenging and you have a tendency to fall back on your career, which feels more comfortable.

Aries North Node, Libra South Node – With your North Node in Aries your True Purpose is going to be in a leadership role or perhaps as a trailblazer. The emphasis in this lifetime is to develop a sense of self as an individual, whereas your previous lifetime, as indicated by your South Node in Libra, was focused on partnership and relating to others. It is important that you concentrate on yourself and where you are going. You need to trust, follow your instincts, push your boundaries, and break through your limitations. Independence and individuality are going to be key to your mission. With your South Node in Libra, you are more comfortable being in a partnership. In past lives this has worked well for you, so it may be difficult to break out of that role. You may find yourself looking for validation from others or trying to fit in and please others. You will feel more empowered when you learn to trust and honor yourself as an individual and a leader.

Taurus North Node, Scorpio South Node – With your North Node in Taurus it will be important to you to feel secure. Having a solid financial basis and stability in your life is going to be significant in your True Purpose. Your Purpose may also include creative pursuits. One of your Life Tools may be that you are practical. However, with your South Node in Scorpio, you may revert to the way you were in a past life, which was more emotionally charged, passionate, and intense. In this life your downfall may be that you can get easily frustrated and overly emotional. A Scorpio South Node may also cause you to be suspicious about others. You will feel more empowered when you are being more practical, grounded, and learn to trust in yourself and others, while not being so drawn in emotionally.

Gemini North Node, Sagittarius South Node – With your North Node in Gemini your True Purpose may involve writing, public speaking, being sociable, and living life to the fullest. You are all about communicating and getting the word out. You may make a great speaker, journalist, author, or publicist. You are also about loving life and having fun. You enjoy new experiences and gaining knowledge, but often have a short attention span. With Sagittarius in your South Node you are the born adventurer and love to travel. You may be scared to be tied down and worry about losing your freedom. Perhaps you are rigid in your beliefs or your philosophy on life. Understanding that truths can come in different forms will help you to grow. Learning to communicate effectively and bringing that into your True Purpose is going to be fulfilling for you.

Cancer North Node, Capricorn South Node – With your North Node in Cancer your True Purpose will likely involve being nurturing, caring, and open to emotional connection. Your Purpose may be reflected in home and family. If it is reflected in your work, then you may be a nurse, caregiver, or generally help others. With your South Node in Capricorn, previously your career came first. In this lifetime you may feel torn between family and career. Because you concentrated on a powerful career in a past life, that's what comes naturally; you instinctively feel good focusing your energy on work. To empower your True Purpose you need to express your loving, caring side and find balance between your home life and career.

Leo North Node, Aquarius South Node – With your North Node in Leo you stand out as a charismatic figure. Your True Purpose is going to be something that allows you to shine and express your generosity. You have a huge, warm heart and connect deeply with people. Your Life Tools may include courage, strength, self-confidence, and creativity. However, with your South Node in Aquarius you are not used to having the attention focused on you. In the past, you've been part of a group identity and not in the forefront. You also may have difficulty relating to people on an individual basis and may try to keep yourself somewhat detached. To empower your True Purpose you will need to learn to take center stage more and connect with people in a heartfelt and genuine manner. When you can get over your fears and stand up as the charismatic figure you are, you will feel more empowered and closer to your path.

Virgo North Node, Pisces South Node – With your North Node in Virgo your True Purpose is going to reflect your talents of logic, analysis, and applying knowledge and training. Your mission will surely be a serious one, as you don't do things casually. Your Purpose may be reflected in teaching or research. You would also do well at writing, particularly non-fiction or technical. However, with your South Node in Pisces you are more used to working from instinct, being creative and not caring about organization or details (or perhaps even leaning toward escapism). You will feel empowered in your Purpose when you learn to use your practical resources in your life and career.

Libra North, Aries South – With your North Node in Libra your True Purpose will involve expressing one's self through relating to others. This may include creating or working in relationships/partnerships/collaborations. Your Life Tools include abilities as a mediator or counselor. In a past life your South Node was in Aries, so you are used to going it alone. Previously, you mastered being independent, coupled with an instinct to be competitive. There is still that residual inclination to be self-reliant as well as to put your own needs first. However, the more you work on and embrace partnerships and collaborations, and finding balance within them, the more you will feel that you are on your True Purpose.

Scorpio North Node, Taurus South Node – With your North Node in Scorpio you are on a journey of transformation. Your Life Tools may include intelligence, wisdom, knowledge, and experience. You are a great motivator and can assist people in deep transformation. Your Purpose may be spiritual. You would do well as a psychologist. As you step into your True Purpose, you may have to shed the material side of your life that you brought in with your South Node in Taurus. Your True Purpose will involve continuing change and flexibility. It will bring energy and passion. You may find it scary to shed your security and material attachments, but this will be a part of your empowerment and coming into your True Purpose.

Sagittarius North Node, Gemini South Node – With your North Node in Sagittarius your True Purpose may be reflected in seeking knowledge (e.g., in academic, religious, philosophical, spiritual areas, or the truth in general). This pursuit may also lead you to travel and seek adventure. Your Purpose may be as a pioneer to define new boundaries. You may also be a teacher/professor, philosopher, or inventor. Your love of travel may be a part of your Purpose as well. With your South Node in Gemini you may have a hard time staying focused and on track as you are easily distracted by the next new and interesting experience. You will need to stay focused and centered to keep on your True Purpose.

Capricorn North, Cancer South – With your North Node in Capricorn your True Purpose may require devotion and durability. You take your role very seriously and are ready to stick it out and endure through difficult times. You actually like difficult situations that challenge you. With your South Node in Cancer, in a past life, your family came first. In this lifetime, if your career takes you away from home, you may have a conflict since you may prefer to stay home with family. Alternatively, perhaps you are emotionally dependent on others. A key component of a Capricorn North Node is to learn self-reliance and true responsibility.

Aquarius North Node, Leo South Node – With your North Node in Aquarius your True Purpose will likely reflect service to others. Often this is within communities, groups, or for a cause. When you are truly on your path, you are not about yourself as an individual, but rather you are focused on the group or humanity in general. With your South Node in Leo, you were used to focusing on yourself as an individual. Having all eyes on you or being in the limelight is something you were accustomed to. Previously, you needed to be the center of attention, seeking acknowledgment and approval, but in the life, be careful not to make it about you. You will feel more connected to your True Purpose when you understand that a group is made up of individuals contributing for the betterment of all.

Pisces North Node, Virgo South Node – The North Node in Pisces is about developing faith and a direct connection with Source and not getting mired in doubt, worldly logic, or over-analyzing (which are connected to the South Node in Virgo). Your Purpose may also involve healing or taking care of others, perhaps as a doctor, nurse, or caretaker. With a Virgo South Node, you are used to living in the world of the physical, the intellect, and valuing perfection. You can be very hard on yourself. Piscean forgiveness and compassion can soften the Virgo criticism (of self and others) and perfectionist streak. Your challenge is to temper the tendency to only focus on the physical realm and embrace your spiritual connection with the One. Understanding that the physical plane is simply an aspect of the spiritual is key to aligning with your True Purpose.

What does the placement of your North Node say about your possible True Purpose? Does it appear to be part of one of the Themes that you're working this life?

_____

_____

_____

_____

_____

_____

_____

_____

What does the placement of your South Node say about your possible previous True Purpose? Is it something that seems to come easily to you or seems familiar?

_____

_____

_____

_____

_____

_____

NUMEROLOGY AND YOUR TRUE PURPOSE

Just as you are born under astrological configurations that match your True Purpose, you are born with numerical vibrations that fit as well. We'll be using numerology to see how it relates to your Life Tools and the True Purpose Statement that you've written.

Your birth number is determined by the date you were born and it has a specific vibration or personality type. Another way of looking at this is that you have a certain personality type associated with your date of birth, which is also reflective of your Life Tools.

Your birth name also has a vibration that is determined by the numerological value of the letters. This is certainly not a coincidence, as we choose our date of birth, astrological chart, and name before we decide to incarnate, all of which support our True Purpose. Of course it all fits; it is Divinely guided.

You are now going to calculate your birth and name numbers to see if they are in sync with your Life Tools and True Purpose Statement.

Simple Birth Number

The easiest and most basic numerological analysis is your Simple Birth Number, which is the day you were born. (Note—The Simple Birth Number uses only the number of the day, not the month.) If the date is a double-digit number, add the digits together to get a single digit number. If necessary, add them again (see the example below).

If you are born on:
July 6th, then your Simple Birth Number is 6
May 14th, then your Simple Birth Number is: 1+4 = 5
March 28th, then your Simple Birth Number is: 2+8 = 10 (then add again) 1+0 = 1
October 29th, then your Simple Birth Number is: 2+9 = 11 (then add again) 1+1 = 2
My birthday is December 16th, so my Simple Birth Number is: 1+6 = 7
Now calculate your own.
My Simple Birth Number is _____

True Purpose Number

Your True Purpose Number is your destiny and it represents your main Life Purpose. Some call it your Life Path Number. To find your True Purpose Number you will now be adding the month and year of your birth to your calculation. However, make sure to calculate each unit (month, day, year) separately before adding them all together.

For July 6th 2001:

Month		= 7
Day		= 6
Year	2+0+0+1	= 3

Now add the resulting digits:
7 (month) + 6 (day) + 3 (year) = 16. Then reduce to a single digit: 1+6 = 7

The True Purpose Number is 7

For May 14th 1978:

Month		= 5
Day	1+4	= 5
Year	1+9+7+8 = 25	= 2+5 = 7

Now add the resulting digits:
5 (month) + 5 (day) + 7 (year) = 17. Then reduce to a single digit: 1+7 = 8

The True Purpose Number is 8

For March 28th 1954:

Month		= 3
Day	2+8	= 10 = 1+0 = 1
Year	1+9+5+4 = 19 = 1+9	= 10 = 1+0 = 1

Now add the resulting digits:
3 (month) + 1 (day) + 1 (year) = 5

The True Purpose Number is 5

For October 29th 1998:

Month	1+0 = 1
Day	2+9 = 11 = 1+1 = 2
Year	1+9+9+8 = 27 = 2+7 = 9

Now add the resulting digits:
1 (month) + 2 (day) + 9 (year) = 12 = 1+2 = 3

The True Purpose Number is 3

There are also Master Numbers, such as 11 and 22. When your result is one of these two numbers, you will not be adding the digits together. Leave this result as a double-digit number. The following birth dates are examples.

For August 19th 1946:

Month		= 8
Day	1+9 = 10	= 1+0 = 1
Year	1+9+4+6 = 20	= 2+0 = 2

Now add the resulting digits:
8 (month) + 1 (day) + 2 (year) = 11 (Master Number–Do not reduce further)

For July 6th 1935:

Month	= 7
Day	= 6
Year	1+9+3+5 = 18 = 1+8 = 9

Now add the resulting digits:
7 (month) + 6 (day) + 9 (year) = 22 (Master Number–Do not reduce further)

My birthday is December 16th 1964

Month	1+2 = 3
Day	1+6 = 7
Year	1+9+6+4 = 20 = 2+0 = 2

Now add the resulting digits:
3 (month) + 7 (day) + 2 (year) = 12 = 1+2 = 3

The True Purpose Number is 3

Now calculate your own True Purpose Number

My Birthday: _____

Month	_____
Day	_____
Year	_____

Now add the resulting digits:
_____ (month) + _____ (day) + _____ (year) =

My True Purpose Number is _____

Numerology of Your Name

Your birth name (the name on your birth certificate) has a vibration determined by the numerological value of its letters. I find that the following is the easiest and most accurate calculation:

Numerical Value	Letter
1	A J S
2	B K T
3	C L U
4	D M V
5	E N W
6	F O X
7	G P Y
8	H Q Z
9	I R

My name is calculated as follows
g a i l   t h a c k r a y
7 1 9 3   2 8 1 3 2 9 1 7 = 53 = 5+3 = 8

Calculate the numerological value of your name (as on your birth certificate) below:

___
___
___
___
___
___

This is how others will see you. If your name number happens to have the same value as your True Purpose Number, then people will see you as you really are.

You may find that the numerological analysis of a nickname or a name that you use other than your birth name resonates better with your True Purpose. You can consciously choose a variation of your name that puts its vibration more in sync with your True Purpose. For example, does using your middle name or middle initial on documents or in your career result in a number that resonates more?

You can also use numerology to influence the vibration of the name of your business. Perhaps you want to alter this name slightly to be more in sync with your numbers. Your business name will also work well for you if it has the same numerological value as your True Purpose Number or your name number.

Look up your numbers and their vibrational meaning below. Do they make sense and relate well to your Themes, Life Tools, and True Purpose Statement? The numerology of your name is going to reflect your personality and the Life Tools you possess. The number of your birth is going to show the vibration of your True Purpose.

THE VIBRATIONAL MEANING OF NUMBERS

–1–

People born with a number 1 are ambitious and creative. They are pioneers and leaders but can be obstinate and domineering. Their drive to accomplish enables them to overcome any obstacle; nothing will stand in their way once they commit to a goal. They may also be physically strong. They will usually stand out as an individual leader rather than part of a team. This is a great number to start a new project or to begin something new. A person with a number 1 has a True Purpose that may include leadership, innovation, and being a trailblazer.

−2−

People born with a number 2 make great partners. They are sensitive, perceptive, diplomatic, and prefer a harmonious environment. They are creative but not overly assertive in putting forth their ideas. As a love interest they are romantic and sensitive to their mate's needs. Their Life Tools may include being a good friend or partner. This is a great number for a collaboration or an agreement. A person with a number 2 has a True Purpose that may lie in being in a partnership (business or personal) or being a mediator.

Surprisingly, sometimes a number 2 will have difficult relationships. This may happen when the person's True Purpose does include having a wonderful relationship, but they first need to learn through experience, what that means. So, in this case, the person may not experience harmonious relationships until later in life.

−3−

People born with a number 3 are great communicators, so they generally do well in a business that involves social interaction, whether one-on-one or among many. They make great speakers, authors, actors, and musicians. Being very sociable, they are charismatic, self-expressive, and optimistic. They may also work in the media or advertising. Another aspect of the number 3 is they are also here to have fun, experience joy, and often help others to do the same. A person with a number 3 has a True Purpose that may include creative expression, social interaction, inspiring others, or helping people experience the joy of life.

−4−

People born with a number 4 are practical, hard-working, trustworthy, and willing to persevere to find success. Giving up is not part of their vocabulary. They approach things in a very practical, realistic, and pragmatic manner. A number 4 prefers to work as part of a group or team, with well-defined responsibilities. They are also are a very loyal friend, partner, or co-worker. Honesty and integrity is a cornerstone for them, but they need to take care that they don't become too rigid in their viewpoint. Their True Purpose may include using their Tools and hard work to build a secure foundation through which they can help others. They bring ideas and plans into physical form.

–5–

People born with a number 5 are impulsive, risk takers, and they make money quickly. They also rebound fast after a setback and nothing seems to bother them. They are freedom-loving, restless, and adventurous. Sensory experiences are an important part of their enjoyment of life. They also make friends easily. The number 5 is good when spontaneous, visionary, or versatile action is needed. Their True Purpose often includes channeling their impulsive, adventurous nature, or perhaps it involves their striking ability to motivate others to achieve success.

–6–

People born with a number 6 tend to be very loving and family-oriented. They are known to give comfort to those in need and are natural nurturers. Making friends comes easily to them and they are very loyal. The number 6 is good number for family, caring, and loving energies, as well as creative and artistic endeavors. They make kind, loving parents. A person with a number 6 may have a True Purpose that is in the creative arts or involves children, family, or helping others.

–7–

People born with a number 7 are analytical, introspective, and independent. They lean towards spirituality or religion but have their own particular ideas. They often delve into the mysteries of life seeking wisdom and truth. Although 7s can be charming and are good in front of an audience, they also need their solitude and alone time. However, they need to be careful they don't become too much of a loner. The number 7 is good number for analysis, observation, and has a keen intellect. You don't accept things at face value but instead do your own investigation into its greater meaning. A person with a number 7 may have a True Purpose to be a philosopher, scientist, inventor, engineer, lawyer, mystic, clergyman/woman, spiritual leader, writer, charity worker, or work in the travel industry.

–8–

People born with a number 8 are often materially successful, having a talent for business and finance. However, they also can be obsessed by money or appear cold and/or lonely. The number 8 is the number most often associated with business, success, and manifesting money. Those with an 8 can be extremely ambitious, attracted to positions of leadership and influence. This number has the potential for great accomplishments, if so desired. The life of a person whose True Purpose Number is an 8 may revolve around money, success, power, or having an influential role in society.

–9–

9 is a number of completion. People born with a number 9 are humanitarians, selfless, compassionate, and want to help make a better world. Many healers, teachers, or spiritual leaders have a 9 vibration. They also make excellent judges, environmentalists, or even artists. The number 9 has a great energy for completing projects. Their destiny is often to complete something in this life or to finish their True Purpose in this lifetime. Often this Purpose has a component of service to others or the world.

–11–

11 is the most intuitive of all the numbers. Insights and awareness come easily. Those with this number are spiritually aware, visionaries, and very charismatic. Many prominent figures in history have this number. There is great potential, ambition, and drive, but one must take care not to be indecisive, self-critical, or lack confidence in one's abilities. 11s are also sensitive, having a natural understanding of others, being able to read people's relationships, situations, health, etc. They are dreamers and deep thinkers. Their path may include being a leader, inventor, artist, teacher, writer, musician, or mystic. The True Purpose of a person born with a number 11 may be to help heal others and the world through their gifts.

–22–

22 is considered the most powerful of the numbers. This is the number of the Master Builder. A person born with this number has the potential to make their dreams and ambitions a reality. They are a powerful force and can achieve great things. They have an innate talent to manifest thoughts and ideas into the physical realm. Care must be taken not to become dictatorial, controlling, or overbearing. They make good business leaders, politicians, and overseers of large projects. The True Purpose of a person born with a 22 number may involve making an impact on the world for its betterment.

Does Your Astrology and Numerology Fit Your True Purpose?

What did you discover about your True Purpose from your astrology and your numerology? Did you discover that these vibrations match your talents, themes and True Purpose and, therefore, help you in pursuing your path? Or did you find where you might have challenges along the way? Did this give you insight into to what aspects of your personality may help you and what aspects test you? Describe what you have learned about yourself.

_____

_____

_____

_____

_____

_____

FINAL TRUE PURPOSE STATEMENT

Your True Purpose Statement

Now that you've completed all the exercises, it is time to finalize your True Purpose Statement. You may want to meditate on it one last time or contemplate your final wording.

My True Purpose Statement is:

_____
_____
_____
_____
_____
_____
_____
_____
_____

You are going to keep referring back to this statement to reinforce what your subconscious needs to do to keep you on track. You are going to say your True Purpose Statement often and out loud. The Universe will support you in your True Purpose. As you regularly say your True Purpose Statement and daydream about it, the Universe will open doors for you.

TRUE PURPOSE IN YOUR JOB AND ACTIVITIES

How Are You Currently Living Your True Purpose?

Now that you have found your True Purpose, what do you want to do? Do you want to quit your job? Move to another country? Start a fresh, new life? Don't worry, you don't have to be that drastic! This is about what you can do to bring more of your True Purpose into your life. The more time you can spend in sync with your True Purpose, the happier and more fulfilled you will feel. However, don't expect to be living your True Purpose every moment of every day. In fact, this may be near impossible.

It is great if your job fulfills your True Purpose (part or much of the time), but sometimes this is just not practical. It is okay if your job is not completely in sync with your True Purpose. Sometimes your job simply pays the bills, and you live your True Purpose through activities outside of work. For instance, it may be through your hobbies, pastimes, volunteer work, and your family. You also have lesser Purposes to work through as well as karmic situations. Your current job may be addressing those, rather than your main Purpose.

How are you currently fulfilling your True Purpose? Does your job fulfill it some or most of the time? Does your home life fulfill it? Are you doing activities through which you feel that you are living your True Purpose? Note how you are currently living your True Purpose.

_____

_____

_____

_____

_____

_____

True Purpose through Career

Since most people's job or career occupies a large percentage of their time, it is an important area to consider. If you've found that your job is already fulfilling your True Purpose, that's great. It is then pretty easy to analyze the connection. In general, if you love your job, it is probably in sync with your True Purpose. If you don't like your job, then it is probably not fulfilling your True Purpose enough or at all. But perhaps there are parts of your job that you love, despite the aspects that you don't really like. For example, you may love interacting with customers, but you don't particularly like the bookkeeping side of your job. Perhaps you love the creativity and artistic thinking that goes into your projects, but you dread making presentations to clients.

If you feel that your job does not fulfill your True Purpose, then it is also possible that you aren't being as productive. When you are working in a way that fulfills your Purpose, not only will you be happier and accomplish more, but others in your workplace are going to be happier as you will likely be better at what you do.

Review your job and/or career. Is there a way that you can do more of what you love and less of the part you don't like? Can you outsource or completely do away with the unpleasant tasks? Even though you don't enjoy a particular task, there may be someone else who would very much enjoy it.

At first glance, you might think there is no way to make changes and that you are stuck with the unpleasant side. However, the Universe is going to support you in what you want to manifest. Think about what aspects of your job you enjoy and what parts you would like someone else to enjoy. Start putting the changes you desire out to the Universe. For example, put out to the Universe that "I am going to spend more of my work time doing [insert what you enjoy about your job] and someone else is going to help me and love doing [insert disliked tasks] of my current job." Start daydreaming and visualizing how this might happen.

Make some notes to the Universe about how you would like your job/career to change to be more in line with your True Purpose.

_____

_____

_____
_____
_____
_____
_____
_____
_____

The 80/20 Rule

There is an old rule of thumb in business called the 80/20 Rule (also known as Pareto's Principle), which basically says that 80% of the result is from 20% of the input. For example, 80% of a company's revenue comes from 20% of its client base. Another illustration would be 80% of a business's complaints come from 20% of its customers.

Look at your job. Is there 20% of your job that you love? This is probably the 20% that is in sync with your True Purpose. Is 80% of your time spent dealing with difficult business aspects or things that you don't enjoy? Does that 80%, which you don't enjoy, really only bring in 20% of your income? Think about this ratio. Does it apply to your job? Does it apply to your career? Does 80% of the pleasure in your job come from only 20% of what you do? If so, how can you get rid of the 80% of the work that really doesn't bring in much enjoyment or income?

Is your job with a client-based business? I bet that if you look at the best paying customers, this small group brings in most of your profit and may also be the least troublesome. Alternatively, the bigger chunk of your time is often dealing with troublesome customers who bring in a small portion of the income.

What if you could change this? Could you literally stop dealing with certain customers who are not worth that much effort? Could you cut out that area of your career that brings in much less in return (both in term of happiness and income)? Where does the 80/20 Rule fit into your job, career, or life? Write some notes to the Universe about what you want to change and how you are going to do that.

_____

_____

_____

_____

_____

Should I Quit My Job?

Some of you may now be looking at your job and realizing that it offers very little in regard to your True Purpose. You may even be saying to yourself, "Oh, this is why I don't like my job!" You are probably also saying that you need it to pay the bills. Perhaps you are stuck in a situation due to familial obligations or other conditions. What should you do? You have found your True Purpose and it is not being fulfilled by your job. Should you quit? If you are independently wealthy or you can easily find a new job in a completely different field that fits you perfectly, you may be able to just up and quit. If that is the case and you are suddenly realizing that you are in the wrong career, great! Do it!

However, for most people it is not that easy. Don't worry. You don't have to go to the extreme of quitting your job. First of all, are you sure that your current job in no way fulfills your True Purpose? It doesn't have to be the actual job that does this; it could be through your co-workers or clients that you get closer to your True Purpose. If your Purpose is to bring humor to people so they can laugh and feel better and there is no humor or joy at your workplace, can you provide this to your co-workers or clients? It's easy to see what parts of your job are more fulfilling as you simply like those parts more.

Perhaps you are perfecting a Life Tool that you are going to use in the future. If you want to become a great fashion designer but right now you're disgruntled because you are working in a fabric store, shift your point of view. You may actually be perfecting your skills to understand what clients like and their needs, which you will use later. If you can understand how you are working to perfect your Life Tools, you will feel more fulfilled.

What can you do in your current job to feel more fulfilled? Can you change positions within your company? Can you rearrange your job to take on more of the tasks that you like and less of what you don't like? Remember, it's not like you are giving all the "bad" stuff to someone else. Even though there are tasks that you don't like doing, there are other people who really do enjoy them. Then start dreaming and planning what your next step is going to be; the Universe will support you. When you start to set your thoughts to what kind of career you would like, what changes you wish to happen, things will start to magically line up.

Don't think that you would never be hired for a job that you desire or that a particular job is unattainable. Many times we are the ones who put obstacles in our own way; but when we really start to reflect on them, they are not as big as they seem. When you take them one at a time and don't give power to your fears, these obstacles can disappear rather quickly.

The way the Universe works is that when you put out to the world what you would like to manifest, the Universe brings it to you. You just need to not let doubt or negative thinking seep in. The best way to manifest is to daydream. Through daydreaming you are putting out visual images and thoughts along with wonderful feelings of excitement for what you are going to be doing and how your life will look. Then the opportunities will start to arise. The Universe will start to open doors for you. Of course, you have to be ready to say "yes" and to go through these doors. So when you are daydreaming about what you want, also start putting out feelers, take action, and say yes to opportunities that come your way.

So what revelations have you had? Are you going to look for a different job? Are you going to alter your current job? Are you going to change careers? Are you going to start a business on the side? Write some notes to the Universe about what your plans are and what you need help with.

_____

_____

_____

_____

_____

_____

_____

_____

In-between Jobs?

Some of you may be having difficulty finding a job. Perhaps you have recently found yourself unemployed. To be honest, this happens more often than not for a reason. Life changes, especially big ones like losing your job or being out of work, are very difficult, trying circumstances. I'm not taking this lightly, but sometimes there is a reason. Often when an extremely difficult change presents itself in our life, it is a challenge for us. Many times it is the Universe kicking us out of our secure zone and making us fend for ourselves to grow spiritually and move on.

Sometimes we are reluctant or scared to change. We may not like our job or our relationships, but we stay because they feel secure or familiar. It's like a baby bird standing at the edge of the nest. It wants to learn to fly, but it is much safer just to stay put. Then suddenly the mommy bird nudges it off the edge and low and behold, it can fly; it soars more beautifully than it could have imagined.

That is us sometimes, standing at the edge of the cliff, longing to fly. We know what we want, but it is still feels safer just to stay where we are. So if the Universe just kicked you out of your nest, it is your time to fly. If you've lost your job, use this as an opportunity. Soon you'll look back saying, "If I hadn't lost my job, I never would have done [____] and I never would have reached my dreams."

It may be hard to have faith, especially if finances are extremely tight; but treat this as a new, fresh opportunity. View it as you've been given a fresh start. Plus, now you know what your True Purpose is. You've been given the time to start planning what you would really like to do. So have faith that you can manifest the career of your dreams and take advantage of the free time you now have; it won't last forever. And daydream! This is a very, very powerful tool. Think in ways you might not have before. Daydream about what you want to do because you are very lucky the world is wide open for you.

What is your perfect career? What action are you going to take to bring it closer to you?

_____
_____
_____
_____
_____
_____
_____
_____
_____
_____

Baby Steps

Let's say you've decided that you need a change of career. Even if are doing what you can to live your True Purpose more fully in your current job and are making the most of your time to prepare your skills, you may know that ultimately, you want a new career. So, how do you do this? As I said before, some of you may have not only the courage but the means and the position to simply be able to leave and start over. But most of you will have a more difficult time than that.

The first thing you are going to do is to start daydreaming. Spend every minute you can telling the Universe what you want your new career to look like. Post photos of things that you want and words that help you to feel your dream job. Put them on your computer, your desk, or anywhere that you can look at them often.

Is there a way that while continuing in your current job, you can also start doing something on the side that is more in line with your True Purpose? Let's say you are in an office job and long to be in the field of natural healing. Can you take some classes to acquire the necessary skills and knowledge? How about starting a small, part-time, sideline business from home? Do you have a friend you can partner with so you both can support and encourage each other? How about volunteering on weekends with a group, business, or individual in the field that you aspire to work in? Don't worry about whether this sideline opportunity is a way to pay the bills because you still have your "day job." Think about ways you can get your feet wet and begin working toward your desired job or career.

The most important thing is to start taking those steps. The Universe will support you and open new doors but only when you show that you are serious. You need to actually take a baby step first. Write down the steps that you are now going to make and note when you will begin.

_____
_____
_____
_____
_____
_____
_____
_____
_____
_____
_____

Your True Purpose in Your Hobbies and Activities

Although your career is a large part of your life, you can also live your True Purpose through your hobbies, activities, and things you like to do with family and friends. Write down how your True Purpose is currently reflected in your hobbies and other activities.

_____
_____
_____
_____
_____
_____

Are there ways in which you can better incorporate your True Purpose into your hobbies and other activities? Is there a class you've been wanting to take? How about volunteering or mentoring? What activities could you do with friends and family where you feel like you're being of service and living your True Purpose?

_____
_____
_____
_____
_____
_____

Check That Your True Purpose Is Actually Yours

When you were young, was there a career path that you were expected to take? What did your parents want you to do or become? Were you encouraged to live your dreams? Or were you influenced by other's careers or their likes and dislikes? Sometimes we follow in our parent's footsteps because we truly want to. Other times we do something to please another.

Think about how you have been influenced by your family and friends and then look at your True Purpose Statement. Is there any part of your statement that is someone else's influence and isn't actually part of your own Purpose? If you were directed by another toward a Purpose that feels right and you know it's what you want, that is fine. But what if it doesn't resonate? If you realize that you've been influenced in a way that is not in synch with your True Purpose, then what adjustments are you going to make?

_____

_____

_____

_____

_____

_____

_____

When you start living your Purpose, the one that is really *your* True Purpose, those around you may change. The Universe works to bring people into your life who support your dreams. New people may show up to assist you. Anyone that is not serving you, but instead is hindering you, may disappear from your life. For instance, difficult co-workers who played office politics to your detriment either suddenly become supportive and helpful or they get transferred out of your department. Perhaps the guy you've been seeing, who has been controlling and disrespectful, no longer seems desirable, and you decide to stop dating him. When you are in alignment, the Universe brings people who will be beneficial and gives you the strength to get rid of the ones who aren't.

If following your True Purpose means going against the wishes of your parents or family, at some point you may have to make a choice because those around you may not support your decisions. When you truly make the choice to fulfill your

True Purpose, you will know that you've made the right decision, and those near and dear may just have to accept it. Many times people will adjust to your choices, and it turns out fine. If someone is truly controlling and stopping you from living your dreams, then this is not a healthy situation and eventually things will come to a head. Ask the Universe for help and support, and it will be provided. Make some notes to the Universe if you think that you need assistance.

_____

_____

_____

_____

_____

RELEASING OBSTACLES

Dictated by Circumstance

Have you felt like your choices were dictated by circumstance? For example, you may be temporarily helping a family member and feel unable to follow your own path. Perhaps you've even given up your career because a spouse or partner asked you to. Have you put everything else on hold while you are raising your children? Do you have other commitments that you feel come first?

Perhaps you think that you could only make a bold move with the support of your spouse. Or do you feel like you need the financial support of your family to be able to make significant changes? You may get this support, but if not, the Universe will provide for you in other ways. Trust, put it out there, and it will come. Do not lock yourself into thinking that help can only be from a particular person or in a specific way. In doing so, you are limiting the possibilities that you are working to create.

In what way do you feel your True Purpose is hindered by circumstance (if this is the case)? Make some notes to the Universe if you think that you need help and support in shifting this.

_____

_____

_____

_____

_____

I've Made a Bunch of Mistakes

Now you have a clearer picture of what you need to do, but perhaps you are concerned with what you view as past mistakes. It is only natural to look back at some of your choices, wishing you could go back in time and change things. Maybe you regret certain decisions. Do you feel like you'd give anything to be able to change history, to not have done something or said certain words? After all, it was totally off your True Purpose. But is that really true? No, of course not. Every choice you've made in the past was absolutely what you were supposed to do. Every "mistake" you made was an opportunity to grow and learn.

Everything we do is by Divine guidance. Even though we have free will, every moment we experience, we are doing so under guidance. What you did is exactly what you were meant to do; so don't live in the past or in regret. You made exactly the right choice for your soul's growth in every action that you took.

If you did something that seemed to be the opposite of your True Purpose, then perhaps at that moment, you needed to see this other side so you could strengthen your journey. Release any feelings of guilt from things that you did in the past, and know that they were exactly what you were supposed to do for yourself and all others with whom you interacted. Live in the now, moment by moment, trying your best to be on your True Purpose but knowing that everything you do and everything that is done to you is Divinely guided.

So what "mistakes" are you going to release from your life? Write them below. Ask the Universe to dissolve them and to remove any associated guilt or fear.

_____

_____

_____

_____

_____

What Is Holding You Back?

If you are not there yet; if you are not completely living your True Purpose in abundance, what is holding you back? Do you have fears about success? Are you scared to go for what you want? Are you afraid that you may fail? Do you feel like you can only get so far and then a block will appear, which prevents you from reaching the top? When you think about your True Purpose do any fears or disempowering thoughts and beliefs come up? Are they blocking or stopping you from living your Purpose? For example, do you think that you cannot make enough money to support yourself if you follow your True Purpose? Do you feel that you don't have the talent to succeed?

Make a list of anything that you feel is stopping you. Even if you can't put your finger on exactly what it is, try. Include your blocks, fears, and negative beliefs. The following is a list of examples. Mark the ones that you feel apply and add any new ones that you have identified.

- I'm always left behind.

- No one helps me, and I can't do it on my own.

- I don't have enough time.

- I don't deserve to be successful.

- I've never been able to achieve my dreams; maybe I'm not worthy.

- I'm not skilled enough; I would need to go back to school and can't.
- I can enjoy myself later in life; I have too many responsibilities now.
- I don't have enough energy to accomplish what I want.
- My health is too poor to be able to do anything with my life.
- It wouldn't be fair for me to take that job as others deserve it more.
- I need to take care of everyone else first.
- I don't have the financial support to follow my dreams.
- My family would reject me if I did that for a career.
- I would like to do this, but it involves public speaking, and I can't do that.
- I'm not talented enough to succeed.
- I would love to take that job, but I can't travel/move due to family.
- Every time I try, I fail.
- I'm afraid of feeling stupid.
- I'm afraid of being judged by others.
- What if I fail? It's better to not even try than to fail.
- I feel prevented by my family/spouse/parents/…
- I can't do that on my own.
- My True Purpose is too big and out of my reach.
- I feel safe in my job even though I hate it.
- I come from a poor background and am not meant to have money.
- Having money is bad/unspiritual/elitist/selfish.

_____

_____

_____

_____

_____

_____

_____

_____

_____

When you actually write down your fears and blocks, you often will find that they are not all that insurmountable. Do some soul-searching to figure out how you can overcome any of these difficulties. After all, you were given this True Purpose by the Divine. You were given all the Life Tools that you will need to follow your Purpose as well as to overcome all obstacles.

Sit quietly in meditation and ask your guides for help in dissolving any blockages. Ask yourself, "When did I create this block or fear?" If you find that it was created in childhood, such as something your parents told you, imagine reliving that moment but now changing it to a more positive outcome. For instance, let's say you would love to travel but you have a fear of it instilled by your mother. She had the attitude that women should stay home and take care of the children and traveling is unsafe or a reckless thing to do. Now reprogram those thoughts. Think about the moment your mother said or did something that instilled this fear in you. Now this time see how it was her own fear, her own upbringing. Imagine having a conversation with her about her fears and releasing them. In this new memory you are creating, tell her how wonderful it would be to travel, and see her being very supportive and enthusiastic of your traveling. You can use this technique to reprogram your negative beliefs from both childhood and your more recent programming.

Remember to ask for spiritual help, as well, to release your fears and blocks. Sit quietly talking with your guides, and ask them to help you to identify and remove your blockages.

PAST LIFE BLOCKAGES

Past Life Regression

Some of our fears and blocks actually stem from previous lifetimes. These can be difficult to identify. You know that you have something holding you back, perhaps you even know the specific fear, but you have no idea where it comes from. Past life blocks can be just as strong or even stronger than a fear originating in this lifetime.

The question is how to address this. Some people have spontaneous memories of past lives. Mostly, though, we can discover our past lives through meditation or light hypnosis. We can specifically ask our subconscious to take us to an event or time so we can see where our block or issue originated. Often just seeing where/how this "feeling" or energy originated will release the issue. Past life regression can also give us confirmation of our True Purpose as we can see ourselves along the same journey in a previous life.

Examples of blocks and fears – Client Sessions

Dan

Dan had a knack for finance and investing and worked in the banking industry. He felt that his True Purpose was to direct people to invest their money in a spiritually-consciousness manner. However, many times his clients didn't want to follow this same philosophy, and he'd feel betrayed. Because he needed their business, Dan felt that he couldn't afford to be picky when choosing his clients. Dan continued to be upset that the majority of his clients simply wanted to make the most money possible and had little regard for the business and moral ethics of the companies in which they were investing.

When we did a past life regression exercise, Dan saw himself as a wealthy merchant. He made loans to local businessmen but only those who he knew had the means to repay him. One day his family came seeking money for his sick niece. She needed a medical procedure and would have to travel to see the doctor.

The merchant refused, arguing that she would never be able to pay him back. His niece ended up dying, and his family never forgave him.

As you can see, Dan had brought guilt from a previous life into this one. This guilt was directing his drive for his current True Purpose. But it was also blocking him as well, such as making him want to control people's actions. He was subconsciously attracting clients who were not of a higher-consciousness mindset in an effort to "teach himself a lesson."

We asked to leave these experiences and the associated guilt in his past. We also asked to now bring through his talents and positive attributes but to leave any negative thoughts in the past. We cleared this negative past life energy and released its associated karma. Dan found that he was no longer so controlling in trying to direct his True Purpose and was now attracting more spiritually conscious clients. The last time we spoke, his business was flourishing.

Jenny

Jenny is a chiropractor who also has a strong intuitive side. All the members of her family are doctors or hold other positions in the medical field. Jenny's chiropractic practice is mainstream and accepted by her family. When Jenny came to me, she felt that her job was her correct True Purpose, but she wanted to include more intuitive, natural work into her practice.

She knew that she was quite psychic and could often diagnose people while they were simply sitting in her waiting room. Still, she was afraid that she would be ridiculed and even struck from the medical board if she pursued this intuitive side. She thought her father's attitude may have contributed to this fear. He raised her to be a doctor, and he thought that anything not scientifically proven was a bunch of rubbish. She loved her father very much and wanted to please him.

Jenny was probably correct that her father's views had instilled this fear of using her intuitive side in her medical practice. When we did a past life regression exercise, we found that it was much more than that. We identified a lifetime during the time of the witch-hunts. Jenny was literally being chased through the streets by an angry mob accusing her of witchcraft. But the most surprising revelation was that the head of the group was her father in this lifetime!

We were able to clear off and release the energies from this past life, leaving any fear of persecution in the past. Jenny went on to incorporate intuitive and natural healing into her practice. In fact, many clients came to her for this very reason—her intuitive abilities. Jenny felt much more fulfilled in her career. Surprisingly, her father was quite supportive as well.

Dillon

Dillon was a great inventor. Even as a child, he had a knack for building things and understanding how things worked. He believed that his True Purpose was hidden somewhere in this ability, but he never could attain the success he desired. Dillon designed equipment for a living but had not received the individual recognition that he deserved because he worked for a large company. He had tried starting his own business but never seemed to be able to get his ideas to market. On top of that, he had been ripped off by others who had essentially stolen his designs. At this point he had shelved his inventions and was working a different job that he found very unfulfilling.

When we did a past life regression exercise and asked to find the source of this blockage, he found himself in ancient Egypt. He had been involved in the design of the Egyptian pyramids. However, because each pyramid took so many years to build, he was never able to see even one completed. He never received recognition for his contributions during that lifetime; he had simply died long before the projects were completed.

I guided him to feel the multitude of people who later came to see his pyramid and stood in awe. He visualized the gratitude of those who for generations have admired his work. Now he was able to leave this feeling, this energy, of not being recognized in the past. We replaced it with the feelings of appreciation.

PAST LIFE MEDITATION TO DISCOVER YOUR BLOCKS

This meditation is to help you to connect with your past lives to discover your blocks and release them. Think about the blockage or difficulty that you would like resolve.

Prepare – Find a place where you can meditate quietly without being disturbed. Sit comfortably (but not lying down where you might actually fall asleep). Light a white or a purple candle and place it in front of you.

Protect – Visualize a bright star in the sky and this star's white rays of light beaming down over the top of your head. Imagine this white healing light coming down over your shoulders, slowly down your body, and completely enveloping your entire body in pure white energy in the highest of goodness. Then imagine tree roots of white light going from the soles of your feet down into Mother Earth. You are now protected in this bubble of white light energy where only good energies can come into your aura.

Breathing/Relaxation – Sitting comfortably, place your hands, palms upward, on your lap. Concentrate on your breathing, taking a deep breath in from your nose, holding it for a second, then exhaling long and forcefully through your mouth. With each breath in, concentrate on bringing in beautiful white light. With each breath out, envision releasing negative energy and relaxing deeper and deeper.

When you are ready for the meditation, you may begin. (You may want a friend to read this aloud to you or familiarize yourself first so that you don't need to read this during the meditation.)

PAST LIFE MEDITATION

Feel a column of white light coming down through your Crown Chakra, running through your body, opening and lighting up each of your chakras as the energy passes through. Then see the white light coming out from your feet and going down into Mother Earth, grounding you. Imagine that your angel or spirit guide is standing behind you, protecting you as you go on this journey.

Now imagine that you are standing at the top of a flight of stairs, looking down. Create this in your mind as vividly as you can. What are the steps made of? Are they wood? Do they have carpet? Is there a handrail? Look down these twenty steps. At the bottom of the staircase is a door. Visualize this door as vividly as possible.

You are now going to walk down the staircase. As you go down, you are going to go deeper and deeper into your subconscious. Count backwards from twenty, going one step at a time, knowing that you are taking a journey deeper and deeper inside yourself. Twenty, nineteen, eighteen…

Now you are standing at the bottom of the staircase looking at a door. Behind the door is another time. You are completely protected with your spirit guide or your angel by your side. When you are ready, open the door. At first you will see a mist of white light. Step into the mist of white light knowing that you are completely protected. As the mist dissipates, you will find yourself in another time, in another life.

Look down at your feet. What do your shoes look like? Or are you barefoot? Look up your body at your clothing. What kind of clothes are you wearing? Are you a man or a woman? (You may be either; your current gender doesn't matter.) Get a feeling of who you are and what era you are in.

Now look around. Where are you? Are you outside or indoors? What scene do you find yourself in? Are other people present or are you alone? What is going on? What are you doing? How do you feel? Even if you are alone, do you feel happy, anxious, sad, etc?

If this moment does not seem to have any importance, imagine that you then go to a different moment during this same lifetime where something important is happening. To do this, focus on this intention, count from one to ten, then look around. Now who is there? What is going on? Imagine yourself in a scene. Remember, you have asked a question about a particular block in this current life. Allow yourself to visualize the scene in which you find yourself. Feel the emotions. Visualize the people around you, and allow your scene to play out. Perhaps you will see an important event or that you're following particular career. Ask your guide if the people you are seeing are also in your current life. And, if so, who are they now?

If you feel scared or uneasy, know that your guide or angel are by your side protecting you. You cannot be hurt; this is in the past. If you visualize a difficult scene, relationship, or feeling, ask that you now release any ties and karma from this past life. Ask that all negative feelings and issues of this past stay in this past lifetime and do not follow you forward. Ask that you fully understand and absorb the lessons from this lifetime and that you no longer need to continue those feelings. Forgive any people in the past that hurt you in that life. Sever any ties that are tethering you to any negative thoughts, situations, or relationships.

Ask what you can learn from this past lifetime about your True Purpose. Ask that any blocks from this past life that are currently holding you back from your True Purpose to be revealed and released. Send love to yourself in this past life.

Now it is time to come back. You'll want to return slowly. Go back through the door you originally visualized. You are now at the bottom of the staircase. Count forward, one to twenty, as you go back up the stairs. One, two, three… With each stair you climb, know that you are releasing all problems, issues, and concerns.

When you reach the top of the stairs, imagine that you are now in your mother's womb. It is your birthday. You are about to be born into this lifetime. Imagine yourself coming down through the birth canal. Imagine that you have all the talents, Life Tools, and wisdom that you will need for your True Purpose. Imagine that you are free from all blocks. You are excited to be born into this life. Imagine taking your first breath.

Now see yourself back inside your body today. You are back, awake, and ready to live your True Purpose. When you are ready, slowly open your eyes. You are now awake, refreshed, free of all blocks, and excited to live your True Purpose.

What did you experience? Did this meditation reveal anything about your True Purpose? Did it reveal the source of some of your current blocks? Did you discover anything that you were afraid of that is currently holding you back? Did you find any other reasons that you can't fully express your True Purpose? Note what you discovered about your True Purpose and what blocks or fears might be holding you back.

_____

_____

_____

_____

_____

_____

_____

_____

_____

_____

_____

_____

Now compare this list to your previously identified fears and blocks from the *What Is Holding You Back* section in the "Releasing Obstacles" chapter. Were any of those fears and blocks also shown to you in your meditation?

Write the specific fear or block that came up in both. These are areas that you may want to put added focus on releasing.

_____

_____

_____

_____

_____

_____

Write a note to the Universe and for each fear or block, sit quietly and ask for it to be released. Afterward, when you think about these blocks or fears, do you feel less worried about them? Do they seem to have lifted?

IMAGINING YOUR TRUE PURPOSE

Now that you have released your blockages from this lifetime and past lives, it is time to give energize your True Purpose.

Your Perfect Day

Now we are going to do a little daydreaming. Sit quietly and relax. Imagine your perfect day. Start by seeing yourself waking up and then going about your day. See yourself being busy, doing your perfect job, having your perfect relationship, or doing whatever is important to you. This is your ideal day so fill it with your favorite dreams. Although being on vacation or lazing in the sun doing nothing may be your first instinct, don't choose that unless you can find a specific Theme in it. Instead think about the perfect "work" day. (I'm using the term "work" loosely. Some of you may be full-time parents, volunteering, etc. Think of this as your perfect "non-leisure" day.) What are the main activities in your ideal day?

_____

_____

_____

_____

_____

_____

_____

The Completion of Your Life

Imagine yourself at the completion of this lifetime. You have lived a long, fulfilling life and have succeeded in achieving all your goals and desires. You lived your True Purpose to its fullest and were greatly admired. Now you are in the afterlife, proudly looking down at the people attending your wake, listening to what they are saying about you and your achievements. You can even read what they've written in your memorial book. What would you like most to hear or read? What would you like most to be remembered for? Imagine your life as having fully lived your True Purpose.

_____

_____

_____

_____

_____

_____

Gratitude in Your True Purpose

When we appreciate something, we send a message to the Universe that we want more of what we are thinking about. If we act in gratitude for something we would like to have, even if we do not yet have it, our subconscious doesn't know the difference and will bring us more of what we are grateful for.

I want you to imagine as if you are already completely living your True Purpose and that this is bringing you great happiness. Now send a message to the Universe that you are grateful. For example, say, "I am grateful for my True Purpose that's been chosen for this life as it is perfect for me." Be grateful for having the skills to carry out your True Purpose. Be thankful that you are seeing signs every day that you are on your True Purpose. Think about living your True Purpose right now and be thankful to God, the Universe, and everyone around you who supports you in your Purpose.

Write down what you are grateful for and whom you are grateful to for helping you on your path.

_____

_____

_____
_____
_____
_____
_____

It is important that you take the time to give thanks for all that you have. When you live in a state of gratitude, you actually attract more for you to be grateful for. Appreciate each moment in your life. Give thanks to all the things in life, not just those that are part of your True Purpose.

In the space below, give thanks to the Universe some of the other things that you are grateful for.

_____
_____
_____
_____
_____
_____

IN SUPPORT OF YOUR TRUE PURPOSE

Make Time for Your Purpose

Most people live life always looking to the future rather than living in the present. Do you ever tell yourself things like, "I will make time for myself when the kids are grown" or "When my husband doesn't need me as much, I can start doing what I want." Do you say that you can start…when…if…after….

You have been given a very big, important mission in life. Your mission is not to put everything aside and help everyone else first. If you have found that helping everyone else is your mission, then it's fine, but this is unlikely. You don't have to give up all your responsibilities, but you absolutely have to carve out some time to do the things that are important to you. What if you died next week and hadn't yet started on your Purpose? How are you going to explain that one?

You need to spend at least some of your time making a start on your True Purpose. If you don't, eventually you may come to resent your spouse, kids, or whoever else your time is focused on. Plus, they subconsciously know your mission as well, and if you're not following it, a part of them will also resent your relationship. When you are living your True Purpose, everyone in your life will be much happier, believe me. Are you familiar with the saying, "what you resist, persists"? If you don't show good faith to the Universe, pretty soon the mommy bird is going to come and push you off that cliff!

This doesn't mean to disregard your obligations, but instead reflect on how you can complete them and still have time for yourself. Is there a way to get help? For instance, can you pool resources with another parent? Look for ways that you can live your True Purpose while still fulfilling other obligations.

If this section applies to you, note what areas of your life that you need help with. How can you consolidate or get help with your obligations? How can you carve out the time for yourself?

_____
_____
_____
_____
_____

You Deserve To Be Successful

You were given a Purpose by the Divine. Stop thinking that big dreams are for others and that you have to take whatever life dishes out to you. Your True Purpose is just as important as those who are famous, wealthy, extremely successful, or extraordinarily beautiful. You have a Purpose—a very big, important Purpose!

You are also not defined by or limited by the circumstances of your birth. You don't have to be born wealthy to be successful in life. There are many well-known successful people who came from impoverished or challenging backgrounds. It is not uncommon to see very successful people who started with nothing.

It's not about how much money you can accrue either. Many will receive great abundance from living their True Purpose, but this is a side gift, a happenstance that often occurs. Those who live their True Purpose love what they are doing. Financial success is often just a byproduct.

Don't ever think that your dreams should not be as big as other people's dreams. If you can visualize it, then it's yours for the taking. The Universe supports everything you desire. We are not in competition with one another. Abundance is infinite, not finite. There is no limit on the number of people who can have similar True Purposes, though most of our desires will have subtle differences anyway.

If this section applies to you, then how big can your True Purpose manifest in your life? What is your biggest dream? Now dream even bigger. Think crazy big and write it all down.

_____

_____

_____

_____

_____

_____

You *Can* Make Money Doing What You Love

Don't ever tell yourself, "I could never make money doing what I love." Of course you can! What do you love to do? Do you love photography, art, or writing? Then start right now. Don't think: "How am I going to make money at this? How is this going to be a job?" Start with things like: "I am going to do this. I am going to be successful at it. This is going to become part of me."

Think of ways to get noticed. Who would love your work? Maybe give it away for free to start. For example, many professional photographers started by taking pictures at local events and just displaying them. I once read an article about a woman whose dream job was to travel and take photos. She started taking photos and submitted them to an airline, simply asking if she could receive a free flight in return for their using her photos from the trip. They loved her sample photos and agreed to her proposal. Now she flies around the world taking photos of exotic locations. The airline covers all her expenses, including first class accommodations, and they even pay her a salary on top of that! She is living her dream job.

Think of ways to make your dream job happen. Do you love to organize but can't get anyone to hire you? There are plenty of charitable organizations that need such help. Many jobs start out as volunteer positions and become great paying careers. Do you love making jewelry, greeting cards, or other crafts? How about doing a side business online from home?

Have you ever heard the saying, "Do what you love and the money will follow"? It's true that when you are living your True Purpose, the Universe supports your desire and everything lines up to help you; but you have to show the Universe you are serious and take that first step!

How can you start doing what you love without worrying about the money?

_____
_____
_____
_____
_____
_____

IT IS YOURS BY DIVINE RIGHT

As you finish this workbook, some of you may say that you would love to do what you came up with as your True Purpose but that it is just a dream. You may think that you need to work at doing something you don't like to pay the bills, that you can only dream about living your True Purpose but never actually be able to do it. Perhaps you think that you don't deserve such a fulfilled life. Do you feel that others deserve that kind of a life, but you could never afford to quit your job or you don't have the talent to pursue your passion?

Remember, your True Purpose is yours by Divine Right. You decided on this path along with the Divine. The Universe supports your dream. The Universe provides everything you need for that dream as long as you pursue it. In fact, when you do pursue it, you will find that doors open and things actually become smoother as you go with the flow of your True Purpose. This is your Divinely-guided life and it is exactly what God wants you to do. Remember, God wants you to have everything that you dream of. What you want, God wants you to have.

WE ARE HERE TO LIVE OUR TRUE PURPOSE IN ABUNDANCE

Get rid of the notion that you don't deserve to earn money from something that you love to do. Jettison the false belief that your True Purpose is to serve spiritually and anything that is spiritual will not pay the bills.

I DESERVE TO LIVE IN ABUNDANCE.

This is so important that you need to post it everywhere and repeat it aloud often. We need to have money to have the experiences that we yearn for and to do many of the things we desire. Our True Purpose is what we are good at. It is where our skills and talents lay, so of course it is natural that we should receive money for it.

It is true that not all True Purposes are fulfilled from a paying job. Some are fulfilled through family and friends, charitable endeavors, or other pursuits. But more often than not, if we are working a job and we are on our path, it will involve our True Purpose either fully or it'll reflect it in a significant way.

I am sure that you've heard the saying, "Do what you love and the money will follow." This is very true and it means: find your True Purpose, do what you are Divinely guided to do, and the Universe will take care of the finances. When you are doing what you love, there is a certain trust in the Universe that attracts money and all that you need. Learn to trust in the Universe more and more.

SPIRITUAL HELP WITH YOUR TRUE PURPOSE

Before you go to sleep at night, when you are in that half-awake, half-asleep state where you are close to your spirit guides, ask them for help. Ask them how you can be more in alignment with your True Purpose. For example, try asking:

How can I bring happiness and abundance into my life while living my True Purpose to [insert your True Purpose Statement] in my highest and best interest?

Do this every night before you go to sleep until the answers start to show up in your daily life.

The following meditation will also help you to receive guidance from your guides about your path and living your True Purpose.

MEDITATION – GUIDE ME ALONG MY PATH

Find a place where you can meditate quietly without being disturbed. Sit comfortably but not lying down where you might actually fall asleep. Light a white candle and place your candle in front of you.

Visualize a bright star in the sky. See its white rays of light beaming down over the top of your head. Imagine this white healing light coming down over your shoulders, slowly down your body, and enveloping you completely in pure white energy in the highest of goodness. You are now protected in this bubble of white light energy where only good energies can come into your aura.

Concentrate on your breathing, taking a deep breath in from your nose, holding it for a second, then exhaling out long and forcefully through your mouth. With each breath in, envision beautiful energy coming into your body. With each breath out, envision releasing negative energy and relaxing deeper and deeper.

Feel your spirit guides sitting by your side. Imagine your main guide and then other guides who are helping you with your True Purpose. Now place yourself in the near future. Imagine that you are living your True Purpose. You have the perfect career, the perfect life work, your perfect joy, etc.

Now you are going to imagine your perfect day. Don't pick a relaxing day at the beach. Pick a day doing the job/career/charitable pursuit, etc. that you envision as your True Purpose. You wake up. It is a beautiful morning, and you feel amazing. How excited are you for what is in store this day? Imagine going through the different activities of your day. Where do you work? What do you do? Who do you meet? And, especially, how do you feel? Spend as long as you can envisioning every detail, really cherishing and feeling how happy you are. Envision returning home after the day's activities. What other wonderful things do you still have in store? What are you looking forward to in the near future?

Appreciate your guides who are with you, alongside for the ride, and so proud of you. Feel the love they are sending. Thank them for helping and working with you. Ask if they have a message for you. Listen for an answer. Ask them to guide you, from this day forward, to be on your path.

Now it's time to come back to the physical realm. Slowly see yourself back sitting in your own room. Imaging a white light that goes down through your spine to the ground, keeping you firmly grounded in this world. When you open your eyes, you will feel refreshed and ready to take on your life challenges, knowing that your guides are always with you. Now slowly open your eyes.

MY NEW LIFE — LIVING MY TRUE PURPOSE

We are all born to experience love, joy, and happiness through our True Purpose. This is your birthright. It is yours by Divine Right. So what are you waiting for? Start living the life you've always wanted!!!

You have discovered your True Purpose! Give yourself a big, congratulatory round of applause! You've identified and confirmed the amazing talents that you've brought into this world. You now know the unique abilities you possess and the special gifts that you are bringing to the world. You are here to help and inspire people through the work you love to do. You now know your importance to the planet and the importance of your existence.

It's time to take action! From everything you have learned, write your top five action points that you are going to do RIGHT NOW.

Action Points I Am Going To Do Right Now

_____

_____

_____

_____

_____

_____

Now it is time to start living your True Purpose.

Today is the first day of the rest of your life. Make a commitment that you are now living your True Purpose and actively enjoying life. Place the following affirmation where you'll easily see it. Repeat these words often.

I am living my True Purpose to [insert your True Purpose Statement]. I am perfectly aligned with and on my True Purpose. I am Divinely guided and live my True Purpose in abundance.

ACKNOWLEDGMENTS

With deep appreciation, I thank the following people:

Most importantly, my family: my Mom and my girls, who believe in me and support me through my crazy adventures. For it would not be possible for me to either write or do my work without their beautiful and loving acceptance.

A special thank you to my Auntie Pauline, my Reiki teacher, and her son, my cousin Ric—my spiritual sounding boards.

My dear friend Mara, without whom this book would probably never have been published and those who helped her put this together, particularly Dawn from Teagarden Designs.

To those who created a forum for me, particularly Robert of the Conscious Life Expo, Ken of the New Living Expo, Mark of the New Life Expo, Steve and Megan of Body Mind Spirit Expo, Chandler of Body Soul Spirit, Patricia and Jacquie from Conscious Living Australia and the gang at Whole Life. Sean of Revolution Radio, Dannion who was saved by the light, and Peter for guiding me. TJ for getting the word out and Digby from Avalon for my spiritual bling.

To John of God for the connection and inspiration.

And those dear friends who work tirelessly so I can do this work: Rory, Leah, Cindy, Michelle, Cindy N and many more.

A special mention to my dear friend Mark, who has supported me from the beginning of my journey.

And especially to my spiritual group and friends who have attended, volunteered, and supported me at my events.

But most of all, my deep gratitude to the divine and beautiful spirits who work with me.

And to God, for through God, all things are possible….

ABOUT THE AUTHOR

Gail Thackray is a psychic medium and life coach. Raised in Yorkshire, England, Gail is now based in Los Angeles. She has written several books about metaphysical subjects and spirituality as well as about manifesting and abundance. Teaching workshops on empowerment and spirituality, Gail has touched audiences around the world. She is the host of a documentary series, "Gail Thackray's Spiritual Journeys," where she travels to meet New Age leaders and experience places of great spiritual significance.

Gail prides herself as being very down-to-earth and was entrenched in the business world when at age forty she discovered that she was actually a medium, able to connect with spirits on the other side.

To find out more about Gail's books, documentary series, and workshops, as well as how to see her at a live event near you,

Please visit her website:
www.GailThackray.com
office@GailThackray.com

www.ingramcontent.com/pod-product-compliance
Lightning Source LLC
Chambersburg PA
CBHW081457040426
42446CB00016B/3286